"Entia non sunt multiplicanda praeter necessitatem."
"Entities should not be multiplied beyond necessity."
(Occam's Razor, or The Principle of Simplicity)
—William of Ockham (ca. 1285–1349)

"[The] sense of identity provides the ability to experience
one's self as something that has continuity and sameness,
and to act accordingly."
**—Erik Erikson, *Childhood and Society* (1950);
Erikson coined the term "identity crisis."**

*"La perfection est atteine non quand il ne reste rien à
ajouter, mais quand il ne reste rien à enlever."*
"Perfection [in design] is attained not when there is nothing
more to add, but when there is nothing more to take away."
**—Antoine de Saint-Exupéry,
Wind, Sand and Stars (1939), chapter 3.**

"A brand for a company is like a reputation for a person.
You earn reputation trying to do hard things well."
—Jess Bezos, founder of Amazon.com

"Simple is smart."
—author unknown

"Alan Siegel wrote the book on making the complex simple, and in the process helped build lasting brands across North America. How fitting that he now has his own book!"

—**Craig J. Kelly, Corporate EVP and CMO,**
SunTrust Banks, Inc.

"All corporations have a personality, whether it's schizo-phrenic or manic-depressive, one with high self-esteem or low self-esteem. They are all distinctive. Alan figures out the positives of their beliefs and personality. He is strong-willed, forceful, and good at presenting bold recommendations on his own terms, never exhibiting any doubt in telling clients what he thinks. Alan is wildly determined to succeed in his work."

—**Herb Schmertz, retired director,**
Mobil Oil Corporation, and former head of
Mobil Oil's corporate communications

"As we enter a world where everyone can be a producer and everyone a distributor, branding will be the sole source of survival for companies. No one understands this world better than Alan Siegel, whose ability to 'cut to the chase,' to provide companies a clear path to connect with their target audience, has time and time again proven to be incredibly effective."

—**Gary E. Knell, President and CEO,**
Sesame Workshop

"Alan did an extraordinary job of getting from us what our brand really is—not just doing a logo, but intensifying the corporation's brand depth, bringing out our essence."
—**Eva Hardy, Senior Vice President, External Affairs & Corporate Communications, Dominion Resources**

"Whether visual or verbal, Alan Siegel always finds a way to distill the complicated into a high-impact communication that is both simple and clear. His reputation for plain speaking is matched only by his unwavering eye for the truth of any situation. We can all learn a lot from Alan."
—**Keith Reinhard, President, Business for Diplomatic Action, Chairman Emeritus, DDB Worldwide**

"Alan Siegel has a unique ability to sense, define, and present the essence of a brand, and then move to communications actions that differentiate the brand through clarity, as well as an edge that attracts and sustains attention in our increasingly cluttered world."
—**Stephen B. Bonner, President and CEO, Cancer Treatment Centers of America**

"Long before others . . . Alan spoke of a brand as the sum total of all expressions and experiences—the brand's voice in the marketplace. He argued that the more unique and compelling that voice, the stronger and more value the brand. It is a simple, powerful idea."
—**Claude Singer, Partner, Lippincott Mercer**

"Alan Siegel was present at the creation of the branding movement; indeed, he was the father of the concept of a branding voice, and by focusing on his trademark simplification, has defined a critically important management tool and communications field."

—John F. Burness, Senior Vice President for Public Affairs and Government Relations, Duke University

"Biographies tell us how human beings succeed and fail, thrive and survive. These stories teach us because we cannot fail to find common ground with the subject. Alan Siegel's biography tells the story of a man who became a success and leader in an area of human endeavor that neither he nor his friends expected. It tells the story of unseen but powerful connections between his past and his future. It tells an important story that will comfort and inspire its readers."

—Bob Kerrey, President, The New School

"In an age of corporate double talk and politically correct euphemizing, Alan Siegel has been a welcome cleansing force. He makes sense out of the complex, he is a brilliant wordsmith and a strategic thinker for organizations and individuals. This book is both a basic primer and a graduate course for anyone who takes communications seriously."

—James L. Abernathy, Chairman and CEO, The Abernathy MacGregor Group

✳

Alan Siegel: On Branding and Clear Communications

Alan Siegel: On Branding and Clear Communications

by Louis J. Slovinsky

Jorge Pinto Books Inc.
New York

Alan Siegel: On Branding and Clear Communications

Published by Jorge Pinto Books Inc.,
    website: www.pintobooks.com

Cover design © 2006 by Nigel Holmes,
    website: www.nigelholmes.com

Book design by Charles King,
    website: www.ckmm.com

ISBN-10: 0-9774724-6-9
ISBN-13: 978-0-9774724-6-8

Acknowledgments

I thank everyone who granted me interviews for this book, including those few, who for various reasons, are not identified in the text. You all helped me gain an appreciation of Alan Siegel and his contributions to the art of branding. I owe special thanks to Mary Sauers of Siegel & Gale, a superb traffic controller who always kept me on course; to Linda Raskin, a proofreader and copy editor without peer; to Liz DeLuna, graphic designer and an assistant professor at St. John's University, who compiled an excellent graphic design bibliography; and to my wife, Joan, whose patience is exceeded only by that of my publisher, Jorge Pinto.

L.J.S.

Alan Siegel

Contents

Author's Introduction

This is a book about Alan Siegel, the master brand builder, but it is not a full-fledged biography. As its publisher, Jorge Pinto, puts it, this is a "Working Biography." It selectively explores Siegel's formative and family experiences, his character and temperament, to understand what attracted him to branding, a rarified profession, where he is an acknowledged innovator and leader. But it is more than that: in capsule form, it shows how branding originated and is practiced today. Finally, it suggests that the great brand-makers earn their bones only with the cooperation of great clients, and in this respect the book salutes courageous clients everywhere.

Siegel began in the branding business at precisely the right time. Following a path blazed by Lippincott & Margulies, the pioneer of the field, several consultancies set up shop in the late 1960s and the 1970s to help position or reposition companies and not-for-profits in need of image makeovers. Invariably, the consultancies started out as corporate identity firms, gussying up their clients' external appearance with new logos, new colors, new stationery and sometimes new names. At the end of the exercise, the image engineers handed management a thick, detailed book of do's and don'ts to maintain the integrity of The Identity.

Graphics designers from Yale, Pratt and the Rhode Island School of Design formed alliances with advertising executives, strategists from management consulting firms and public relations counselors to offer what was first called Corporate Identity and has now morphed into Branding. Pure graphic design studios and design gurus abandoned their corporate employers to enter the frothing competition.

Siegel would be the first to say that when he launched Siegel & Gale in 1969 with Bob Gale—who left not long afterward—the differences between his practice and veterans like Lippincott, newer firms like Anspach, Grossman & Portugal, or the firm where he cut his teeth, Sandgren & Murtha, were differences with minor distinctions. They all did pretty much the same thing.

But Siegel was determined to take corporate identity a giant step further. He learned to synthesize solutions for his clients based on their needs, history, ethos, culture, employees, products, leadership and stakeholders, and to contextualize and test his insights against reality. He wanted his solutions to work, be flexible and have the durable legs of a marathoner.

He evolved an analytical—almost psychoanalytical—multidisciplinary problem-solving approach to branding that finds its roots in history but is driven by modern technology and the exigencies of the marketplace.

The antecedents of large-scale branding and integrated corporate identity are legion, if not immediately obvious. Consider the Roman Catholic Church. From its earliest days, the church developed rituals, introduced special uniforms, and adopted a complex table of organization and impressive management titles according to a carefully ordered brand architecture. No organization has better leveraged symbols, architecture, music and language, all forms of communication and persuasion, to make a continuing impact on its constituency.

When an emerging movement is deemed commensurate (aligned) with church intents and values, the church seamlessly absorbs it. The Franciscans coexist with the Jesuits, and the church speaks in one ecclesiastical corporate voice. Certainly this was not a deliberate "communications strategy" at the start, but just as certain, the church has benefited from its dynamic brand, which has stood the test of time, with periodic updates to remain relevant. (Who knows if Opus Dei will outmuscle the Jesuits to become the protectors of the church?)

Throughout history, megabrands ("brands" here applied loosely) have risen and fallen. Some of them evolved organically. Others were appropriated traditions. What unites successful brands is their instant familiarity to the people of their time. They conjure up strong images and associations. They communicate in vivid language, and they all have a distinctive point of view.

As pointed out by Wally Olins, the British brand consultant, modern branding can be traced to the way patent medicines were marketed in the nineteenth century. Coca-Cola famously capitalized on its brand as a mass marketing tool and became the biggest advertiser in the U.S. In short order, cereal producers (Kellogg's), soap makers (Lever Bros. and Procter & Gamble) and countless other manufacturers of everything from household commodities to automobiles began inventing their own brands.

Beyond distinguishing themselves from the competition, brands build consumer trust by representing products of consistent quality and standard pricing. Whether you drink Coke in Atlanta, Des Moines or San Diego, you know how it will taste and what it will cost. (The quality goes in before the name goes on.) Service brands, on the other hand, depend on the character and behavior of the people behind them, which could vary widely. Can the quality of employee actions be controlled like the secret recipe and manufacturing process for a beverage? Perhaps, but it's hard; it's about delivering on one's promises; it's about earning a *reputation*.

In the 1970s and 1980s the notion of branding migrated from massively advertised packaged goods to the companies that made them. Corporations, non-profits and individuals alike were being labeled "brands." As a function of the consumer movement and an increasing awareness of business's social responsibility, a more educated population began looking at the companies *behind* the products. "Who is accountable for products when they fail or destroy the environment?" consumers were asking.

Siegel understood that most corporations "present muddled communications to their customers, employees and other constituencies. [They] haven't developed a consistent and powerful language to define who they are, what they do and what they stand for." Their communications, he said bluntly, are tone-deaf—one can't tell by their overall message whether a company identity is functional or glamorous, elegant or down-to-earth.

Siegel & Gale devised and constantly refined its own fact-based methodology to reveal the special personality of a corporation and the vision it strives for. For part of its existence, the firm called the concept Corporate Voice, a forerunner to its branding approach. The core idea was to work toward a single ideal, an "overarching strategy," Siegel termed it, which guides the implementation of solutions throughout all organizational levels.

He argued for the totality of corporate expression. Corporate Voice is not a logo, a face-lift or an ad campaign. It is not about corporations singing their song at the highest decibels, but rather singing in harmony. Superior skills are needed to vary the modulation of the Voice, to avoid monolithic top-down communication, to make the organization's messages work together and *resonate*.

This slender book shows why Corporate Voice works and why it is one of Siegel & Gale's two great contributions to branding. The other is Language Simplification, the art of using clear and comprehensible language in such documents as income tax returns, loan agreements and "fine print." An idea that truly broke new ground, Language Simplification constructs communication of improved clarity, functionality and honesty to *reinforce* contacts between companies and customers. Above all, simplification offers organizations a powerful, and very visible, tool to manage customer relationships and even buttress customer loyalty. Applying plain English in transactional documents helps "align" (more about that word later) companies with their promises of leadership and customer responsiveness. This may be Siegel's greatest legacy, as it affects so many of us. Siegel & Gale's slogan, "Simple is smart," has always remained a goal worthy of relentless pursuit and, in fact, is the lodestone that guides the firm today.

Like all else in the business arena, Corporate Voice too evolved, and in today's business vernacular is called Branding, a term often ill defined and poorly understood, as Siegel discusses in this book. "Brand" has been appropriated, willy-nilly, and applied to consultants' offerings, their firms' names, to virtually everything. The New York Yankees are a brand, Apple Computers is a brand, and so is Tom Cruise. How can this be? Has the concept of "brand" become perilously denatured by sloppy usage? Siegel holds strong beliefs about this.

And what of Alan Siegel, the subject of this Pinto Books *Working Biography*? He is neither a designer nor a copywriter. According to some, he is only a passable stand-up presenter. He was never formally trained in these skills. Yet he *is* a great communicator, an astute analyst and high-percentage problem-solver. Asked to describe him succinctly, a former Siegel & Gale executive simply says, "Right. He is nearly always right."

The seeds for Siegel's success took root in many places:

In a mother's unconditional love and the example she set. She exhorted her son to aim high, succeed and keep raising the bar.

On the basketball court. A tennis-playing partner, the writer Sidney Offit, suggests that Siegel's taste of athletic stardom during the sports-worshipping fifties was a tonic to his confidence. (It also didn't hurt to be tall and charismatic.)

Behind the camera's rangefinder and in a darkroom making prints. Siegel acknowledges that photography focused his creativity and sharpened his powers of observation.

In his ability to recognize and glom onto golden epiphanies, to take chances, resist conventional wisdom and never shrink from the danger of innovation.

Except for succumbing to the hype of the Dot-Com bubble—who didn't?—Siegel seldom failed to recognize a great idea, his own or others', which if pursued fully and enthusiastically could become business-worthy.

This then is also a story of Alan Siegel: not a household name to the public but a respected competitor to his peers, a man without great family connections, educated belatedly, bankrolled largely on the collateral of his ideas, who becomes a visionary destined to start and run his own enterprise.

In the branding business, consultants claim many of the same clients in their portfolios, because large companies and their subsidiaries tend to request proposals from a small universe of brand experts. But if you ask the paying and pro bono clients, past and current, served by Siegel & Gale over the last 35 years—AARP, Disney, Pitney Bowes, Motorola, Merrill Lynch, American Express, Dell, Dow, Sony, Lexus, Microsoft, 3M, U.S. Air Force, Nature Conservancy, Robert Wood Johnson Foundation, Dominion Resources, Metropolitan Transportation

Authority (MTA), The New School, the Girl Scouts, Sun Trust, Lehman Brothers, Allstate Insurance and many more—you will learn that Alan Siegel's "breakthrough simplicity" contributed tellingly toward building their powerful brands.

Louis J. Slovinsky
Katonah, New York

Chapter 1: Hoop Dreams

An indifferent high school student who did just well enough to be accepted to an Ivy League university, Alan Siegel bet on his first love, basketball, to become his ticket to success. Though an avid reader, he didn't write a great deal or have remarkable skills at communication. This would have shocked his future branding clients, who invariably are mesmerized by his articulate presentations. Indeed, had there been a debating society at his high school, he wouldn't have participated. He just wanted to play basketball, up to eight hours a day, shooting baskets night after night at a hoop erected on the family garage. In the mornings, he would blindfold himself and dribble up and down the street. And on some days, he would tie his right hand behind his back, using only his left in order to develop ambidexterity.[1]

Little in Alan Siegel's youth suggested he would pursue and excel in a highly specialized business career. Like many immigrants, his forebears sought the American dream. His great grandfather was a native of Russia; his great grandmother, of Hungary; his grandparents and parents were American born. Eugene Siegel, his father, spoke some Yiddish, which Alan only discovered when his father was in his eighties.

Gene was a salesman for Knapp Photoengraving, a firm that made copper plates for high-quality four-color advertisements. Photoengraving in the days before the universal penetration of television was essential to Madison Avenue. During the heyday of great print advertising, Gene worked side by side with top ad agency art directors to make plates and proofs, adjusting them to suit the client. For example, he worked closely with the noted art director Henry Wolfe, who, along with Stewart Greene, Dick Rich and Mary Wells, formed one of the great agencies of the day, Wells, Rich & Greene.[2]

"Being timely, being reliable, not bullshitting people, delivering what's promised—I think I learned that from him," Siegel says. Well known and respected by high-caliber ad people, Gene was always on time, straightforward and reliable—qualities the agencies admired. "That's how I was introduced to the advertising business and the graphic arts industry," Siegel adds. His father acquainted him with the plate production process, all the while emphasizing that photography was the basis for it all.

With his father's help, he got a summer job at Gilbert Advertising, whose best-known client was London Fog, the raincoat manufacturer. "The agencies trusted my father," Siegel says. "He was technically sound, reliable, stood up for his clients, and delivered what he promised. He was a very good communicator in the sense that he really understood the graphic arts business."[3]

Siegel's mother, Ruth, was not merely a homemaker but also a community leader. She was president of a Long Island chapter of Hadassah, the Jewish women's charitable service and education organization. Although not college trained, she could deal with well-educated people on an equal footing, became head of the Parent Teacher Association and led campaigns to restore school funding in Rockville Center, where the Siegels lived. An articulate woman, she wrote speeches and represented a "powerful force that people related to."[4]

Alan Siegel was born August 26, 1938, across the street from the Bronx County Courthouse in New York, in the lengthened shadow of Yankee Stadium. The Siegel family moved to Rockville Center when Alan was four. Rockville Center, the seat of Long Island's Roman Catholic diocese, was a suburban community populated with middle-class people, a few professionals, and mostly working families and small business owners.

The only neighbor with any wealth was Ralph Schneider, a founder and later head of Diners Club. Begun in 1950, Diners Club initially targeted its cards to 200 "associates," mostly New York salesmen, who entertained clients at 14 New York restaurants. Within a year, Diners Club attracted a membership of 20,000 and had contracts with 1,000 restaurants. Siegel's father received Diners Club card No. 00064. "When we were in Europe, they wouldn't accept the card and thought it was phony," Siegel remembers. Another resident, who lived down the street, was Harry Henshel, the president of Bulova Corp., the watch manufacturer. The Henshels were the first local family to have a TV set, a Dumont, and occasionally invited the sports-hungry Siegels to watch the boxing matches.[5]

Siegel remained in the community through his sophomore year at Southside High School, until his father's business faltered. Seeking cheaper housing, the Siegels moved to Long Beach, a summer resort town on the ocean side of Long Island. They were crammed into a tiny apartment that accommodated a family of four, including Alan's sister, Susan, now deceased. Later they moved within Long Beach to a small bungalow on stilts over Reynolds Channel. Their next-door neighbor was Joseph Carlino, the Republican Speaker of the New York State Assembly, who was to help the Siegels in time.

Fast Breaks

Unlike Rockville Center, with its neat houses and lawns, Long Beach was funky, its end-to-end beaches swarming with sunbathers during the summer but bleakly deserted in winter. (Like Matt Dillon in the coming-of-age film *The Flamingo Kid*, set in a later period, Siegel worked by day as a cabana boy at the Lido Beach; at night he valet-parked cars at 25 cents a vehicle.)[6] The move to Long Beach, and his switch to Long Beach High, helped cultivate a skill that would pay Siegel dividends for years. At his former school, Rockville Center High, he was at age 14 the first freshman ever to play on a Long Island varsity basketball team. Six feet tall and skinny, he played guard and forward, and competed against 18-year-olds, including Manhasset High School star Jim Brown, who earned 13 letters in five sports and became the greatest pro football running back in history.[7]

At Long Beach High, Siegel played under Robert Gersten, a legendary basketball and baseball player at the University of North Carolina, who remembers Siegel as a strong rebounding forward. Siegel knew Coach Gersten well, having attended the coach's family summer camp in Brant Lake, New York, in the Adirondacks, from age five through sixteen. That was where he really learned to play basketball, competing not only against kids his age but also much older camp counselors who were already playing for major college teams. "My dream was always to go to college on a basketball scholarship," he says.[8]

The one person Siegel admired or paid any attention to in his high school years was Coach Gersten, his "mentor and father substitute." Gersten served as the dean of Nassau Community College until his retirement. Now 86, he still plays a couple of hours a day of tennis and golf, despite two hip transplants. Says Siegel: "He's fantastic, the greatest guy; I'm very close to him."

Siegel's hero in high school was Tom Gola of LaSalle College (1952–1955). Siegel emulated the set shot of the four-time All American, who was drafted by the Philadelphia Warriors. But it was Dick Heylmun, a starting guard with the University of Pennsylvania, who inspired Siegel to play for Penn. At the last minute, however, Siegel changed his mind and opted for Cornell University. Though the young Siegel spurned his alma mater, Heylmun wrote him an encouraging letter supporting his decision to choose Cornell, a university Heylmun regarded highly. When Siegel graduated from Long Beach High, his position on the team was taken over by Larry Brown, who went on to a distinguished basketball career as a player and coach in college, the ABA and the NBA.[9]

Thoroughly Inspired

There was good reason for Siegel to choose Cornell, which, like other Ivy League schools, did not award basketball scholarships: it was less expensive than Penn. He may also have been influenced by Dick Schaap, the late sports broadcaster and book author, who was the editor of the Cornell *Sun*. Schaap, whose mother ran a gift shop with Siegel's mother on Long Island, arranged to have Alan visit Cornell.

Siegel matriculated at the Industrial Labor Relations School, a state school that was part of Cornell. As a state institution, Cornell offered a low tuition for New York residents. The school was founded by an act of the New York State Legislature in 1945 "to improve industrial and labor conditions in the State," through education, research and dissemination of information. Given a home at Cornell, the school describes itself as "embody[ing] both the intellectual rigor of the Ivy League and the democratic spirit of the state universities." It remains the nation's only institution of higher education offering a four-year undergraduate program focused on the workplace.[10]

Cornell's Labor Relations School was the ideal place for Siegel. He could afford it (barely); he could work part-time, in a fraternity house kitchen; he could play basketball; and he had the chance to compensate for his lackluster high school academic record. Although he majored in industrial labor relations, he was permitted to sign up for undergraduate liberal arts courses offered at Cornell. Thoroughly inspired and motivated by Cornell's students, professors—indeed, the whole stimulating campus environment—Siegel plunged into academics and quit the Cornell basketball team after his freshman year.[11]

Critical Thinking

Instead of the customary five courses per semester, Siegel often took six or seven. Besides the curriculum required for a degree in industrial labor relations, he studied art, literature, philosophy and history. Moreover, he was tutored informally by his friends in the evenings. "When I first went to Cornell, I was overpowered by the academics because I really never applied myself in high school," he says. "I really couldn't write well."[12] Fortunately, Robert Dudnick, Siegel's fraternity brother at Zeta Beta Tau, the historically oldest Jewish school fraternity, recognized that Alan was struggling and needed help.[13]

Dudnick had gone to Shaker Heights High School, then Ohio's number one high school, and had a solid background in English. He graduated Phi Beta Kappa from Cornell and earned outstanding grades at Yale Law School. Fond of Siegel, whom he describes succinctly as "charismatic," Dudnick showed him how to outline an essay, diagram sentences and a build a logical and persuasive case—the way Dudnick still does today as a successful Los Angeles litigator.[14] Dudnick's critiques immediately helped Siegel's writing, which he would further refine in law school.

Cornell offered fertile ground for the education of Alan Siegel. He concentrated on improving his critical thinking, reasoning and learning skills. Transformed from a lifelong jock to a passionate student, he now consciously strived to become "a thinking person, a well-read, educated person determined to actively participate in society." In the process of elevating his communication and rhetorical skills, he gained enormous confidence.

Siegel's studies steered him toward labor law, in an era when the union movement was more robust than it is today. Tensions between management and labor were manifold and sharp. President Franklin Roosevelt's secretary of commerce, Frances Perkins, taught at Cornell and became somewhat of an influence on Siegel. Siegel was also taken with Alice Cook, another professor and an important figure in the labor movement, social work and adult education. As the nation's premier industrial relations school, Cornell drew great labor leaders and top government officials for speaking engagements. One of them was former President Harry S. Truman, who gave a three-day seminar in 1960, to which Siegel had the distinction of being selected to attend.[15]

Despite its isolated campus in upstate Ithaca, New York, Cornell was a magnet for outstanding teachers. The faculty included Vladimir Nabokov, whose Russian literature course Alan enjoyed; Arthur Mizner, an F. Scott Fitzgerald specialist; Morris Bishop, a Cornell PhD and professor of romance literature; and Alan Soloman, an art critic who conducted a yearlong seminar on modern art, one of the best courses Siegel took. Overall, Cornell was "just a phenomenal experience."[16]

Cornell's educational style was critical to Siegel's academic success. Students at Cornell were not as pampered as, say, those at Harvard, where it was thought the faculty took pains to pass everyone. Borrowing the lyric from the song "New York, New York," if you could make it at Cornell, Siegel believed, you could make it anywhere. Thus he was aggressive in selecting courses and studying them assiduously.

His fraternity brothers came from good schools and often occupied the top tier of their high school classes. Often the first generation of their families to attend college, they pursued education with zeal. Even at the Greek houses, not known as hotbeds of intellectualism or sobriety, the frat brothers rated the best teachers and touted superior courses, the ones worth a student's major detour. In 1960 Siegel graduated third in the Industrial Relations School and was vice president of the senior class.[17]

Family Values

During summer vacations, Siegel found work through his neighbor New York State Assembly Speaker Joseph Carlino. One job was loading milk trucks from midnight to eight in the morning. He also hauled cement for a construction company and cleaned the Nassau County public beaches. As a teenager he caddied at Rockville Center's country club. No job was too menial.

However modest his parents' means, Siegel was seldom without wheels. His uncle, Arthur Wheelwright, a
self-educated, worldly police officer, managed to find
him cheap used cars from the age of sixteen on. At one
point, Siegel owned a 1950 blue Mercury, which he fancied
resembled James Dean's famous chopped Merc in *Rebel
Without a Cause*.[18] In college he drove junk heaps that
barely made it through the snowy hills of upstate New
York. Wheelwright influenced Siegel in ways uncles do,
teaching him the manly arts of driving and repairing a
car, handling a motorboat, digging for clams and steamers
at Jones Beach, and negotiating the undiscovered sandy
beaches of the Hamptons on Long Island's east end in
an open Jeep. "He was well read and courageous, and
treated me like an adult," he says of his uncle, the former
top motorcycle cop in Nassau County.

Siegel's father was a religious Jew, a member of the
Reformed Temple. Out of respect for him and his father's
parents, Siegel was bar mitzvahed. Actually, he was raised
by Ruth, a doting mother who decidedly was not religious;
indeed, her two sisters married gentiles. Whether Siegel
should or should not have assimilated into the non-Jewish
population never surfaced as an issue. His goal simply was
to become a "top sports person," and his father abetted
that dream.

A savvy salesman, Gene acquired expense account
season tickets to games at the Polo Grounds, Yankee
Stadium and Ebbets Field, and regularly patronized the
old Madison Square Garden on Manhattan's 49th Street.
With his dad, Siegel saw countless games played by the

Giants, Knicks, Dodgers, Rangers and the Rovers (the Rangers' hockey farm club). They even journeyed to Jamaica Arena in Queens to catch the fights and professional wrestling. Father and son were hard-core sports fans, but not necessarily "homers," the fans who root exclusively for the home teams; they applauded all great performances. Alan Siegel's favorite basketball team was the Boston Celtics.[19]

If his father indulged his sports appetite, Siegel's mother commanded the greater influence, teaching the value of hard work and admonishing him to cultivate an unwavering sense of self. That is precisely how she lived her life. A fearless political activist, Ruth interacted with community leaders like Joseph Carlino, the number two man in the state behind Governor Nelson Rockefeller. "My mother ran the show, and my father was kind of a quiet guy," Siegel says. "Her attitude was, 'You can do anything. No one should take no for an answer. Always shoot for the stars.'" Holding education as the first priority, she counseled her son to "go to the best place you can, work hard and read." When she died in 1960, of breast cancer, Siegel was in law school. "Everything seemed to fall apart," he says. Ruth ran the household and kept it together. Her death left a painful hole in his life.[20]

As if responding to Ruth's dictum to "read, read," Siegel read omnivorously during the fifties. He admired the works of Thomas Mann, Thomas Wolfe, and avant-garde writers like André Gide. As well he liked Norman Mailer, James Jones, F. Scott Fitzgerald, the great Russian novelists and the reclusive J. D. Salinger. The irony, he said, was that "you read all these books when you were too young [to fully appreciate them]." Besides the mandatory Cornell texts, Siegel regularly perused *The New York Times*, *Time*, *Life* and the Cornell *Sun*. If he could reprise his life, Siegel says, "I probably would have been a journalist," reflecting his admiration for Schaap, a journalist who, before most of his peers, wrote empathetically about black and women athletes.[21]

Popular culture at Cornell revolved around fraternity parties, beer blasts and movies in Ithaca. On weekends, star performers like the legendary Mississippi guitarist Bo Diddley played the town, along with lesser known touring bands and classical musicians. Remarkably, there were, in Siegel's memory, only a handful of African Americans at Cornell during his time; one of them, Erwin (Bo) Roberson, won the Silver Medal in the long jump at the 1960 Olympics. Only in New York City, where Siegel barnstormed and played on all-star basketball teams, did he meet many African Americans. Attending an Ivy League school in the 1950s, it seemed, had its cultural limitations.[22]

Chapter 2: Picture Perfect

Butzbach, West Germany: 1st Lt. Alan Siegel, age 22, slid to a stop in his used red Triumph TR4 roadster and opened the door for his passenger, a much older German named Georg. The improbable duo was off on a photographic expedition, the first of many, seeking bucolic views for Siegel to record with his new Honeywell Pentax 35mm camera. Wrangling 8-inch Howitzers was hardly boring, but off duty, Siegel grew restless. An ambitious young man not given to wasting time, he took up photography and darkroom technique with Georg. He made photos of military maneuvers and published them in Army journals, which pleased his commanding officer because Siegel's candid shots helped publicize the battalion's activities. This was good for recruitment, good for the CO's ego, and especially good for Siegel. For it was in Cold War Germany during the early sixties that he discovered his creative side. Here he began developing an aesthetic and an analytic acuity that served him throughout his career as a master brand builder; a strong visual sense that guided his life's work helping to reinvigorate the communications strategies of corporations and institutions, their products and services, throughout the world.[23]

A snapshot of Alan Siegel in 1960: tall, gangly, with close-cropped black hair, framing a profile a Hollywood actor could envy, and newly graduated from Cornell; but what next? Because his father and close family friends were not of the professional class, the few business insights he gleaned were from Ralph Schneider of Diners Club. At Cornell, in his junior and senior years, he temporized over what career path to pursue, due in part to the school's inadequate counseling services. He went on no interviews with company recruiters visiting the campus and, in fact, no industry appealed to him. Preoccupied with acquiring a good education, he failed to cultivate mentors to help him enter the world of business.

Almost by default he opted for law school. This was a trying, conflicted period in his life. His mother was dying of breast cancer, and the Cold War armed forces buildup would surely trigger his military obligation. After all, he had completed four years of R.O.T.C. at Cornell and was commissioned a second lieutenant. One sure way to remain near Ruth, in the final months of her four-year ordeal, was to obtain a deferment from military service.

Gene Siegel's health insurance ran out, forcing him to care for his wife at home by himself. With the help of the well-connected Mr. Carlino, the Siegels moved to Peter Cooper Village, a desirable middle-class housing complex on the East Side of Manhattan above 14th Street. Within walking distance of his parents' apartment was New York University Law School, which had just edged into the list of top ten law schools in the U.S. Siegel applied to NYU

Law and was admitted. Naively, he thought that "being in a profession with a graduate degree would set me up for life."[24]

At NYU Law, Siegel learned lasting lessons about writing and thinking clearly, and about himself. But on balance his law school experience was distasteful. Students were lodged in the same seat in the same room every day as professors cycled through to deliver their lectures. It was a shocking contrast to the idyllic Cornell campus. Residually, the law school aspect he liked best was learning to think like a lawyer, working through complex fact patterns to define issues and solve problems. He stayed a year and a half, during which time he watched his mother painfully die. He took a leave of absence from law school with the expectation of returning, and accepted his Army commission in 1962.[25]

Metamorphosis

On the strength of his college math background, Siegel was trained at Fort Still, Oklahoma, the home of the artillery, for a military occupational specialty that required calculating azimuths (angles of fire) and range, fire volume, type of fuse and ammunition, critical adjustments, and numerous details in artillery placement and firing. He might easily have been shipped to South Korea as to Germany, but, fortunately for him, he wound up with the 2nd Howitzer Battalion, 18th Artillery, in Butzbach, a Hessian town of medieval half-timbered houses that has garrisoned foreign troops since the Roman occupation.

The mainstay of American and NATO heavy artillery units like Siegel's were the M115 8-inch Howitzers, which had tactical nuclear capability. Even hurling conventional 200-lb. projectiles, the guns were deadly enough, and accurate; in the right hands they could take out a garbage can at 17 kilometers.[26] The battalion's principal mission was to defend the Fulda Gap, focal point of the largest peacetime concentration of military forces in history. More than one million NATO and Warsaw Pact troops faced off at this strategically important avenue to the Rhine River, waiting for World War III to erupt.[27] It was through the storied Fulda Gap that Germanic tribes flowed to defeat the occupying Roman legions. As a forward artillery observer, Siegel went aloft in a Cessna L-19 Bird Dog, flying low and slow under the artillery arc to spot targets and advise gunners on adjusting their fire.

Siegel had another, self-determined assignment as well. As was common during the Cold War, many "enlisted men" were in fact draftees, and all the officers in the battalion, except Siegel and one other, a Princeton man, were regular army or professionals, cleaving a sharp class divide in their *Kaserne* (barracks). The lower-ranking soldiers—rural kids, minorities from the inner city, resentful and poorly educated draftees—were frequently cited for infractions of Article 15 of the U.S. Uniform Code of Military Justice, usually for misbehavior in local towns. (Article 15, a nonjudicial proceeding, gives a commanding officer the power to punish individuals for minor offenses.) The enlisted men requested Siegel to defend them in Article 15 procedures, and he was so evenhanded that the battalion colonel appointed him the permanent prosecutor for these hearings.[28]

Siegel's sense of generosity and fairness, demonstrated as a young man during his military years, has informed his management style throughout a long business career, according to past and present co-workers. Colleagues say he has the ability to make distinctions in his regard for employees, to value a person as an individual apart from his or her professional abilities. Even when an employee underperforms or is clearly not up to the job, Siegel may not retain him or her on staff, but he can still cherish, show compassion for and help the person afterward—which explains his lasting friendships with those who have moved on, even when they join the employ of competitors.

Self-Discovery

A signal self-discovery during Siegel's military hiatus was his deepening fascination for photography. "Photography opened up my creativity and a whole new side of my personality. [Until then] I never knew I was a creative person. I never thought of myself as a visual communicator or, really, a communications person." (His love of photography continues to this day as a collector of pictures and author of books on photography. *Art & Antiques* magazine, in 2004 and 2005, rated Siegel's collection one of the top 50 collections.)[29]

When Siegel returned to the U.S., he informed his father he was renouncing law school for a career in journalism . . . or, he hesitated, perhaps advertising. He interviewed with the director of *Life* magazine's promotion department, and with *Look*'s editors, the latter offering a plummy entry-level job writing picture captions. Surprisingly, neither of America's biggest mass-circulation magazines of photojournalism appealed. In hindsight Siegel sometimes wishes he had gone into photojournalism. Instead, happenstance intervened. A family member got him an introduction to Richard Avedon, the celebrated fashion and portrait photographer. Siegel showed him his work, and Avedon liked what he saw.

Avedon encouraged Siegel to take a weekly workshop on "concept photography" with Alexey Brodovitch, the Russian-born art director of *Harper's Bazaar*. In his 25-year tenure at America's premier fashion periodical, Brodovitch transformed the art of magazine design with asymmetrical layouts, generous use of white space, and dynamic imagery.[30] Perpetually enveloped in a cloud of cigarette smoke, the Russian master handed out assignments and closely critiqued his students' work, sometimes "tearing people up and down." Brodovitch, Siegel recalls, was interested in new ideas, not pretty pictures, and new ways to express complicated ideas.[31]

Avedon also advised Siegel to study with Lisette Model, the Viennese photographer who famously recorded the raw drama of New York City streets and was now teaching at The New School.[32] For Siegel, the photography courses restored the intellectual challenges and excitement of Cornell. At the same time, his pragmatic nature compelled him to rigorously seek job interviews.

Bette Davis Eyes

Amid his serious pursuit of photography and a position in "communications," Siegel met Gloria Mendel, on a blind date in 1964. A slender woman with long brown hair and Bette Davis eyes, Gloria soon changed the narrative of Siegel's life. A graduate of Denver University, she was in New York working for Robert Evans, a sometime actor who was helping his brother run Evans-Picone, a women's sportswear company. (Evans was to become a producer, then president of Paramount Pictures, responsible for such acclaimed films as *The Godfather* and *Chinatown*.)

Gloria invited Alan for a drink, and they talked for four hours nonstop. "I thought he was the handsomest man I had ever laid eyes on," she says, "and he still is." Well-built, his military haircut growing out thickly, Siegel, to some, resembled Victor Mature, the hunky Hollywood actor of the forties and fifties. Gloria was taken with Alan's self-confidence, his curiosity, and especially his ability to listen intently.[33]

Evans left the garment industry, but Gloria remained in New York, in the employ of Marty Goodman, an agent representing established entertainers the likes of Bill Cullen, Bert Parks, Arlene Francis and Jonathan Winters. In 1965 Gloria married Siegel, and they moved into a small studio on 52nd Street, surviving on salaries of $150 a week each. To enable Siegel to launch his own business, they delayed having children for a time. They have a daughter,

Stacey, who received a fine arts degree from Cornell and worked at MTV and Siegel & Gale. She is married and living in California. The Siegels also took in Charlese Sutton, their housekeeper's youngest child, so she could attend Walden School in New York City. Cookie, as she was known familiarly, was treated as a family member. The recipient of full scholarships from Skidmore College and Hunter College of The City University of New York, Cookie is married and works as a dance therapist.

From the beginning, Gloria became intimately involved in Siegel's consulting business. She supported him in starting up his firm at age 29 when they had no resources. "He was clearly someone who had to lead, not follow, and I admired his drive," she says. Because Gloria had a strong marketing background (she majored in business), Siegel frequently discussed projects to gain her insights. "I worked by his side from day one, whenever he needed me to," Gloria says. "I did naming from the beginning—free, of course—and got Jeff [Lapatine] involved when I was desperate for help with a name." Lapatine, a lawyer by training who was working in what Siegel & Gale called simplified marketing communications at the time, helped Gloria by developing the name CashStream for the Mellon Bank's ATMs, which the client bought and loved.[34]

Today, as a part-time staff member of Siegel & Gale, with the title Co-Director of Naming and Senior Consultant, Gloria specializes in creating names for corporations, subdivisions of corporations, products and services. She works closely with Lapatine, Siegel &

Gale's Group Director, Naming & Brand Architecture.[35] Practitioners of the name game are loath to claim sole credit for developing a new moniker. That includes Gloria, who invented NYCE, the name of a consortium of banks that operates 150,000 ATMs and has issued 60 million debit cards.[36] She protests that a colleague came up with the full name, the New York Cash Exchange, while she "only" reduced it to its acronym. However, it is the acronym that endures, one of many sturdy names Gloria continues to create.

Chapter 3: The Apprentice

Alan and I were the only two guys in the program that didn't have MBAs. We did two-month stints for a year in different advertising disciplines: Health and Beauty Aids, Household Products, Sales Promotion, and so on. You worked on new business pitches or gathered information for them. We were housed in the Information Retrieval Center, which was really storage for magazines, reports, books and a new technology called Xerox machines. The general manager of the program was Hank Norman, a German-born American citizen with an Erich von Stroheim accent who scared the living crap out of everybody but Alan. Alan had just spent two years in the Army in Germany and thought Norman was funny. Turned out that Norman was a pussycat.

—James Kiewel, former Executive Vice President, Siegel & Gale[37]

Feeling clueless about the world of commerce, Siegel joined the training program of BBDO, a respected advertising agency. The hands-on program, both Siegel and his father reasoned, could be an expeditious way to acquire an overview of advertising, marketing, media, design and visual communication. "When I was going through the BBDO training program, I spent all my time with the art directors, writers and TV producers," Siegel says of this opportunity.[38]

BBDO, an important agency with marquee accounts, offered a comprehensive salaried training program that would shame today's business internships. "They were an establishment agency, but I got a chance to learn marketing, media, film production, market research and advertising; to meet important people in the business and see how they did things," Siegel says. Completing the program, Siegel was selected to work with Bruce Crawford, a brilliant business manager with a reputation for being highly organized and productive—"something that was rare in the advertising business at the time," says fellow BBDO trainee Kiewel. "I can't imagine anyone consolidating so many ad agencies, other than him. He was a very aloof but sophisticated figure. His life's dream was to be the general manager of the Metropolitan Opera Company, and he realized it."[39]

In charge of BBDO's major accounts, Crawford rose to CEO of the agency, then vaulted to chairman of Omnicom, the firm that owns BBDO and a host of advertising and media assets. All the while, he was a trustee of the New York Metropolitan Opera Association, a prestigious civic service. He so loved the Met that he left advertising for three years to be the opera's general manager. However, Omnicom had expanded so greatly, its management asked Crawford to return and lead the organization as chairman and CEO. Eventually, he assumed the chairmanship of an even larger world-class performing arts complex, New York's Lincoln Center, while simultaneously serving as Omnicom CEO—an exquisite, and quite possibly unparalleled, balance of two extremely demanding jobs. Today, at age 77, Crawford has geared down only slightly, holding the titles of chairman emeritus of Lincoln Center and non-executive chairman of Omnicom.[40]

Siegel regards Crawford as perhaps the most outstanding businessman he has ever known. A man of icy reserve, Crawford was adept at spotting promising talent and good ideas. Says Kiewel: "To Crawford, it didn't matter who or what you were. If you had a good idea, and he recognized it as such, he'd go with it."[41] Crawford parceled out assignments to the younger staff members to study trends that might materially affect the agency and its clients. Well before the burgeoning of cable TV, Siegel was asked to analyze the new medium, write a report and monitor the industry's development. The information from this and various other internal studies helped Crawford build a knowledge base that ultimately made him the stand-out candidate to head BBDO.

Proof

During Siegel's first year at BBDO, Crawford was in charge of a new product and design program called the Communications Design Center, which created packaging, promotional material and new products literature. Siegel's passionate interest in visual communication oriented him to the unit's quarters in a penthouse originally built for real estate mogul William Zeckendorf, Sr., at 485 Madison Avenue. There he closely observed graphic designers as they worked on new logos, packaging, promotions and in-store displays. He was also fascinated by great art directors sketching out advertising concepts.

Siegel was assigned account executive for American Tobacco Company's Tareyton cigarettes, which ran an extensive ad campaign on network television, spot television, radio, outdoor and magazine advertising. He spent a good deal of time in California overseeing the production of commercials by creative director James J. Jordan, Jr., "a strong-willed, dominating guy," who wrote many memorable product slogans during five decades as an adman.[42]

Employing something he called "nameonics," Jordan linked a product's brand name with its benefits or attributes. Jordan's slogans are legendary in the ad business: "Us Tareyton smokers would rather fight than switch!" "Have it your way with Burger King," "Wisk beats ring around the collar," "We bring good things to life" (for General Electric), "Schaefer beer, when you're having more than one," "Delta is ready when you are," "Quaker Oatmeal, it's the right thing to do," and "Zest-fully clean."[43]

The lessons Siegel absorbed from Jordan were durable, particularly the way he communicated, solved problems and zealously supported effective ad campaigns. "Jordan was passionate about the business, and fought to keep people from throwing away good things to adopt a fad or fashion," Siegel says, an observation that became codified into Siegel's canon of business principles: Always build on a solid asset, and never abandon something that's working, even to please a client. To paraphrase Jordan, Siegel would rather refresh an asset than switch.

On his climb to creative director of the agency and ultimately president of BBDO, Jordan invented the "Blue Skies" presentation to prepare his associates for an ad campaign. It consisted of a big board painted with blue skies and surrounded by fold-back flaps that when lifted revealed key advertising ingredients such as Market Research, Past History, Pricing, etc. When the geometrical exercise concluded, all that was left on the field of Blue Skies was a miniscule square representing "the creative space we have left." In sum, Jordan believed that *all* of the client's essential goals had to be met when creating a solution. Perhaps one could make a lucky stab at the right solution, but the odds were very high against it. As in all geometry problems, points are earned for getting the proof right, not necessarily for the right answer. Clients appreciated the adduction of the "proof," a lesson that resonated throughout Siegel's career.

Siegel was, and is, an intuitive, quick study, with an I.Q. near the top of the chart. The obverse of this innate trait is that his attention span wanes quickly, according to both friends and critics. From the outset he demanded to know *why* his associates proffered a resolution to a problem; what ingredients and reasoning went into the calculus. To him, the proof was golden.[44]

In the sixties, BBDO was a white-bread, old-line ad agency competing against such stalwarts as J. Walter Thompson, Benton & Bowles, Ogilvy, Gray, Dancer Fitzgerald and Sample, and Doyle Dane Bernbach. Siegel

grew bored working on the cigarette account and concluded that the advertising business was "not stimulating."
Nevertheless, he entertained a job offer by Wells, Rich
& Greene on the Benson & Hedges tobacco account.
Eschewing the glamour associated with working for the
much-in-the-news upstart agency run by Mary Wells, he
peremptorily decided it was not a step forward.[45]

Synapsis

Still searching for his own way, Siegel forsook the
Wells, Rich offer, much to the disappointment of his wife
and father, and instead took a position, at less money, with
Ruder & Finn, a public relations firm of excellent repute.
During a year's stay at Ruder & Finn, he quickly learned
how to deal with the media, write press material and run
a crisis management account. In his last assignment, he
devised a press strategy for the Sperry Gyroscope division of Sperry Rand, a large NYSE company, which had
contracted to build a traffic control system in New York
City but couldn't deliver. Sperry hired Ruder & Finn to
minimize possible damage to its reputation if New York
City, as anticipated, cancelled the project.

Siegel researched New York's proposed system for
redirecting traffic with the Sperry engineers tasked with
designing the system. The Sperry professionals concluded
it was impossible to build an effective system as stipulated
in the proposed specs, because the city's unforgiving
grid pattern severely limited alternative routes over its
streets and avenues. Siegel compiled a comprehensive

media package bolstered by diagrams showing clearly how complex the job was—in effect, making the case for the other side of the story to forestall criticism of Sperry. "It was really like a Simplification program [see Chapter 5], taking complex ideas and articulating them in terms laymen and the media could understand," he says. The project was a stimulating experience for Siegel, capping a short but intensive introduction to the public relations business.

Richard Weiner, Siegel's boss and a principal of Ruder & Finn at the time, observes: "The first thing you notice about Alan is that he devoted the start of his career to training with outstanding organizations, which benefited him as he went on to form his own company at a young age. Energetic and enthusiastic, Alan was very good at 'synapsizing,' i.e., connecting his experiences. He has always done that. Alan has been extremely good at recognizing a great idea; it doesn't matter whether the idea was originally his or some else's."[46]

While sharpening his business writing and understanding of the working press at Ruder & Finn, Siegel again gravitated to visual communication, this time in the person of S. Neil Fujita, who ran Fujita Design, Ruder's in-house design shop. A Japanese-American who had been interned in the U.S. during World War II, Fujita is best known for his memorable record jacket designs (Dave Brubeck's *Take Five*, the big-selling jazz album)and book covers (*The Godfather* and *In Cold Blood*). Siegel established a working relationship with Ruder & Finn's staff designers, with whom he collaborated to create brochures, annual reports and information graphics used in press kits.

Breaking Away

In the late sixties and early seventies, graphic design reemerged with a creative energy not witnessed since the Bauhaus. Colorful psychedelic graphics were commodified by the youth culture. Serious graphic designers imported pristine typestyles like Helvetica from Europe, not to mention introducing white space, lots of it, into advertising and editorial pages alike. Firms like Lippincott & Margulies, Chermayeff & Geismar, Raymond Loewy, and Walter Landor, and one-man bands like Saul Bass, imprinted their graphic *dictats* on everything from packages to corporate literature to signage and trucks. Corporations aching to break out of stylistic mediocrity provided plenty of business.

Joshua Gordon Lippincott was trained as a civil engineer but became an industrial designer. He helped design the Campbell soup label, the FTD logo (Florists' Transworld Delivery) and the radical Tucker Torpedo automobile, among thousands of products and logos.[47] With Walter P. Margulies, an architect and astute salesman, the two formed Lippincott & Margulies in 1943.[48] Lippincott & Margulies was responsible for three major contributions to corporate identity: Lippincott himself coined the phrase "corporate identity"; the consultancy pioneered the planned, coordinated approach of expressing a company's corporate identity (though some corporate identity practitioners still insist the methodology simply evolved and cannot be attributed to a single person); and they professionalized the business, relying not on one or two creative stars but on a management consulting process practiced by expert interdisciplinary teams. Certainly, Margulies almost single-handedly instructed corporate leaders on the competitive advantage of a well-defined identity.

Joseph M. Murtha and Russell A. Sandgren, hardly renegades but ambitious and well experienced in corporate identity, were the first to break away from Lippincott & Margulies to start their own business. Specializing in corporate identity, packaging and marketing, the firm billed itself as Sandgren & Murtha. A wit, writing to *The New York Times*, joked that Sandgren & Murtha "sounds more like names seen on trucks delivering cement and rock."[49] But Sandgren & Murtha could deliver the corporate identity goods, and Siegel was actively recruited by the executive vice president of the firm who had been his mentor in the BBDO training program. He joined the firm in 1968.

Sandgren & Murtha introduced Siegel to the world of corporate identity on a comprehensive scale, offering clients research, strategy and high-quality design. The firm created logos and identity programs for the likes of US Steel, Cargill, Metropolitan Life and TransAmerica.[50] Working out of elegant, modernist offices on New York's Third Avenue, Sandgren & Murtha was "doing terrific identity programs for great corporate clients," Siegel says. He managed a number of highly successful projects for the firm, encouraged by the promise of a partnership at the end of a year. The partnership never materialized, ostensibly because Siegel, then 28, was considered "too young."[51] (No matter that the huge ad agency Young & Rubicam had already appointed Steve Frankfurt creative director at the tender age of 32.)

New Venture

Disappointed but undaunted, Siegel began raising capital to form his own corporate identity firm. An initial deal with a wealthy investor with no experience in the field didn't work out. On the strength of some working experience and a modest business plan, he pitched the Venture Capital Group of First National City Bank (now Citibank) and received a $100,000 line of credit—a sum he only partially tapped. Together with Robert Gale, a laid-back designer he met at Sandgren & Murtha, Siegel set up Siegel & Gale in 1969, in a mixed-use building on 52nd Street between Third and Lexington Avenues. Within a year the firm moved across the street to a small penthouse that recently had been renovated by a talented architect who, unfortunately, went out of business.[52]

Siegel & Gale assembled a fledgling staff, people the partners had worked with before. In its infancy, the consultancy signed up clients interested mainly in their visual identities. One of Siegel's early personal triumphs, in 1970, was creating the National Basketball Association logo. The assignment to update the NBA's trademark came through the Licensing Corporation of America, which wanted to increase the appeal (and value) of its NBA licensing agreement. NBA Commissioner Walter Kennedy wanted to relate the logo graphically to the Major League Baseball trademark, a profile of a batter on a red, white and blue field—a design, coincidentally, that Siegel championed when he was with Sandgren & Murtha, and had presented to Mike Burke, who was in charge of promoting the 100th anniversary of baseball.[53] The reason Kennedy sought the stylistic association with America's national pastime is eerily familiar: professional basketball's image was tarnished at the time by drug and labor problems.

Siegel ploughed through the picture files of *Sport* magazine, edited by his boyhood friend Dick Schaap, and selected several that could fill the bill. The one finally chosen by the NBA was of Jerry West dribbling up-court. It became the iconic white silhouette against a red and blue field. Siegel himself cleaned up a tracing of the image, slimming down the figure a bit to work better in various applications. Says Siegel: "This simple, powerful image rocketed off the page and harmonized perfectly with the batter's image in Major League Baseball's trademark. The [basketball] Commissioner selected it immediately. No discussion. No research. No hesitation." The fee Siegel received for his work was $3,500. Today, the logo appears on every piece of NBA-licensed merchandise, which generates $3 billion in annual revenues.[54]

In 2000 Siegel was introduced to Jerry West in a Los Angeles restaurant and the logo was discussed. The former star player was somewhat blasé and not impressed, excited or complimentary about the fact that his image was the basis for one of the world's most recognizable logos. West still claims uncertainty as to whether he was the model for the logo, and the NBA, for reasons unrevealed, won't confirm or deny it.[55] Shortly after David Stern became NBA Commissioner, Siegel ran into him at a Caribbean resort, and they discussed updating the logo. After all, players were now wearing long, baggy shorts, and most of them were African American. In the end, Stern determined that NBA logo was so well accepted by sports fans, a change couldn't be justified, though such a possibility is still debated in the sports press.[56]

Developing logos and visual identities was the sirloin-and-baked potato business of Siegel & Gale in its early years, but Siegel aspired to become more than a "logo and letterhead" shop. He wanted to create corporate identity that was inclusive and comprehensive. He believed the traditional barriers between advertising, direct response, public relations and promotion had to be torn down to deliver truly integrated programs that reinforce a more penetrating identity across all media.

In 1974 Gale, the chief designer, resigned from Siegel & Gale, and sold his share of the firm to Don Ervin, who was Sandgren & Murtha's creative director for nine years. Ervin also brought a wealth of experience as a graphics and product designer for George Nelson & Co., where he worked on the corporate identity of Abbott Laboratories, one of the earliest identity programs. At Sandgren & Murtha, Ervin supervised a staff of 20 and designed or directed scores of major identity programs, including

Transamerica, Cargill and Conoco.[57] Siegel retained the firm's original name, Siegel & Gale, because the firm increasingly was winning visibility in the marketing community and, in particular, was lauded as a pioneer in Simplification, a completely new discipline.

Chapter 4: Classic Identity

When I first started in corporate identity, it was a "silo business"—a very distinct discipline that mainly revolved around graphics. It was heavily skewed to designing logos and design systems. Ad agencies controlled the strategic relationships with the clients. Slowly, corporate identity morphed into branding, and I'd like to think I played a big role in the change. I kept saying, you can't really build an identity without a strategic message, positioning, a voice. The identity firms had direct contact with corporate CEOs, and chief marketing executives took an active role in reviewing research and committing to programs that had more content, more depth, and were more strategic. Advertising agencies, which had a lock on the client relationship when I started in the business, became a commodity business. Preoccupied with producing TV commercials, the agencies continued to make a lot of money, but they lost that gatekeeper role.

—Alan Siegel[58]

In the 1970s, potential corporate clients asked identity firms to present their credentials, occasionally in the presence of the clients' advertising agencies. Sometimes the agencies solicited corporate identity practitioners to act as subcontractors on visual identity issues. To be sure, ad agencies had a vested interest in monitoring and maintaining their client relationships, which often can become frayed.

The onset of negotiated commissions helped loosen the agencies' iron grip; clients took over media buying and to a degree began controlling production of TV commercials. "The best and the brightest, who used to go to the agency side, were now opting for the client side. Eventually the power base shifted, and identity firms were assigned the major strategy work," Siegel says.[59]

No Two Alike

The need for a corporate identity program often is prompted by a defining corporate event—a takeover, merger, rapid diversification, restructuring, deregulation, globalization, technological change, the perceived commodification of a company's products, or the installation of a new management bent on leaving a lasting imprint.

A company presents itself to its various publics through myriads of daily transactions—selling, buying, advertising, informing, hiring, firing, and so on. All these interactions, whether intended or accidental, add up to a corporation's identity. The ability to mold that identity, to make the company's strategy, vision and structure comprehensible and visible, is an indispensable management tool. In the early years of corporate identity, great emphasis was placed on the corporation's name and logo, and on the structure of its identification system, i.e., how the parts related to whole.

Wally Olins, the British identity consultant, parsed the identity of companies into three large categories. Corporate, or monolithic, Identity relies on one name and one visual system in everything a company does. Each subdivision of the company bolsters the others. What is called Endorsed Identity involves the "endorsement" or identification of subsidiaries with the corporate name and its style, a useful strategy in relating acquired businesses to the acquirer. A Branded Identity separates the identities of the parent company and its products. Consumers link psychologically with the products, while other constituents, such as the financial community, identify with the corporation.[60]

These broad categories remain relevant, but corporate identity as now practiced is grounded in more subtle analysis and execution. Competition is more aggressive and the stakes higher than they were a couple of decades ago. Moreover, clients want to confirm that their investment in identity supports their business results.

After a work plan is formulated, consultants gather information about the organization, its component parts and competition. They interview management, employees, customers, vendors, stockholders, stakeholders—those who can best illuminate the company's behavior. They review the client's literature, press, marketing studies and financial analyst reports; the company's positioning, mission, values and culture; its performance and plans. Consultants also conduct original customer research, both qualitative and quantitative, to measure "awareness" (name recognition), so-called familiarity (the degree to which people feel they know a company), and company strengths and weaknesses, as compared with the same attributes of four or five peer competitors.

Researching key audiences helps validate impressions held about a company. Research yields benchmarks that can be replicated periodically to measure a program's effectiveness and provide insights into course corrections. The metrics of "reputation" also suggest whether the public will support a company during a period of controversy or crisis. One of Siegel & Gale's early insights was that employees are the most important audience to probe, their knowledge and cooperation particularly important to creating a strong corporate identity and brand.

The issues and challenges thus defined, the consultants construct identity strategies based on the facts uncovered, taking into account the nature of the company's ownership, its corporate structure, management beliefs and aspirations, and shared organizational values. Key messages, communication strategies and timelines are developed and recommended to management. Alternative solutions, subject to testing, could range from creating a new visual identity, name or logo to devising a new nomenclature system, advertising campaign or employee education program.

Bluntly summarized, the calculus of corporate identity might be misconstrued as formulaic, but it isn't. No two companies are alike, and seldom are the remedies to their problems. The best solutions are company- and market-specific, not riffs on the same melody. Everything on the solutions menu has a price tag, whether bundled into a package or executed on its own. Only when management adopts the findings, embraces the recommendations and fully funds the program does the long march toward a new identity begin.

Defining identity is the first challenge. "Inhabiting" a company through learning immersion, consultants try to understand the organization's value system, which is almost always present, even if management has consciously avoided cultivating a set of shared values. (Avoidance behavior—the unexamined life, Socrates phrased it—signals a kind of studied anti-identity.)

Identity is expressed through a corporate "idiolect," a sort of private language and ethos. To alter, slightly, an aphorism by the writer James Salter, identity (indeed, the brand) is "something valuable, like a dense metal buried in the earth that could guide one's actions."[61] As propounded by Siegel, identity is the *essential truth* of an organization:

> I've always said that my process is geared to drawing out, from the company itself, its history, vision and culture, and the realistic constraints it faces—what they can do and what they can't. In the end we try to come up with solutions that are original and true and can be delivered.
>
> You have to know what's going on in the marketplace, but the customers aren't going to tell you how to position and define your company. Identity has to be based on something concrete, on the company's character. Identity also has to be

visionary and somewhat aspirational. You're not going to get that from the marketplace. That's an important difference between my philosophy and the competition's, and why I've been successful to a certain degree. Companies are complex organisms that can't be condensed into a slogan, as ad agencies do with packaged goods.[62]

A corporation's identity can suffuse and influence lines of business, distribution channels, even the managers of local fiefdoms. When any of these entities "don't get it," the organizational machine may falter. "Getting" the identity depends on crafting clearly defined positioning statements as a platform for solutions offering palpable customer benefits. The positioning must be communicated across a social network sown with minefields of misunderstanding, overcoming all perceptual obstacles to ensure that key slices of the public, starting with employees, understand the organization's identity and promises. The ultimate goal is to methodically build authentic, long-term identity solutions to business problems, not to perform bravura but soon-to-sag face-lifts.

Charter Clients

Not only did some of the Sandgren & Murtha staff join Siegel's fledgling firm, he attracted, almost by default, one of their accounts, Uniroyal, a global company best known for its tires, chemical products and U.S. Keds, the classic athletic shoe brand. Feeling neglected at Sandgren

& Murtha after Siegel left, Uniroyal hired Siegel & Gale several months after the co-partners launched their business. "Sandgren & Murtha never thought Uniroyal was a high-potential or appealing account, but it turned out to be a great account for us," Siegel says.

His first Uniroyal assignment was to design retail stores for its Croyden subsidiary in South America. In 1973, Siegel was asked to redo the Uniroyal corporate identity because of confusion between the corporate trademark and a specialized trademark used by their highly visible tire stores. (Lippincott & Margulies earlier changed the company's name from U.S. Rubber to Uniroyal.) "Bob Gale and I merged their separate corporate and tire logos into a new logo that would function as a master brand for all of their consumer, industrial and tire products," Siegel says. "The fee for the job was $10,000. That job today would be $300,000 to $500,000. But we made money on the project because we sat down in a room, sketched out alternatives and decided on a direction to refine the logo—in 45 minutes."[63]

In the seventies, Siegel & Gale created classic corporate identity programs for Pitney Bowes, Conrail, Tishman Realty Corporation and 3M. Most of these trademarks are still used 30 years later. Take, for example, the Pitney Bowes logo. Siegel & Gale won the Pitney Bowes account in a competition against Anspach, Grossman & Portugal, a perennial rival. Beginning as a postage meter company more than 80 years ago, Pitney Bowes rose to world leadership in providing integrated mail and document management systems and services. The company holds

3,500 patents for mailing, systems engineering and other applications. In 1971 Siegel & Gale developed a trademark for the company that remains fresh and relevant. A cruciform of nesting right angles, the Pitney Bowes mark symbolizes the precise repetition of the postage meter and the company's continuing technological innovation.[64]

The next client Siegel & Gale signed up was Scovill, Inc., an industrial conglomerate based in Waterbury, Connecticut, giving Siegel a chance to work with H. Malcolm Baldrige, Scovill's CEO. Confirmed the 26th U.S. secretary of commerce in 1981 during the Reagan administration, Baldrige hired Siegel & Gale to devise a program to help the secretary's staff simplify the correspondence he had to sign every day—a project that eventually buoyed the credibility of Siegel & Gale's Simplification business.[65]

In Search of 3M

The work Siegel & Gale did for 3M marked a turning point for the consultancy. 3M is a company with more than 60,000 products sold in markets worldwide. Many 3M products are genuine brands, but a large number are SKUs, or Stock Keeping Units, an identifier used to manage inventories. 3M, the corporation, is a *brand*; 3M sandpaper is a *product* and a *brand*; and there are scores of varied sandpaper grits (SKUs) deemed to be separate "products" but not distinctive "brands." All of the foregoing made 3M one of Siegel & Gale's most challenging projects.[66]

Self-described as the "abrasives company," Minnesota Mining & Manufacturing Company used the logo "3M Co." as early as 1906. "3M Co." was set inside a diamond enclosed by a circle displaying the company's full name and Duluth headquarters. The 3M mark underwent periodic cosmetic changes until 1960 when Gerald Stahl & Associates, a New York firm, developed a boxy serif logo that resembled something like an early twentieth-century German industrial firm. The designers worked up a complete font of similar letters for 3M's brand names and signatures.[67]

In *Advertising Age*, in 1961, Joseph C. Duke, a 3M executive vice president, articulated the need for the new logo:

"When one product, division or subsidiary makes a favorable impression anywhere, every other 3M division, subsidiary or product should benefit. In turn, the achievements and prestige of the 3M Company should benefit each product and activity of the company."[68]

3M codified its corporate identification system, replete with a manual to police the use and prohibit abuse of its logo and graphics applications. "By 1965, however," 3M's website states, "faced with an onslaught of brand and package design proliferation, management had a change of heart." The promise of a visual corporate coherence could not be realized as the company's brand and package designs multiplied in the mid-sixties. Another design firm, Brooks Stevens Associates of Milwaukee, was brought in, and they created a color-block system, vaguely alluding to the work of Dutch abstract painter Piet Mondrian, "to avoid design monotony yet maintain an unmistakable family resemblance among all 3M products." One color block identified the product; a second, the division that made it; and the third bore the 3M logo. The system failed to help customers identify the packages as 3M products.[69]

No one was happy with the special typeface created to work with the color system, especially European packagers who needed to communicate in several languages. Reduced to smaller sizes, the typeface was unreadable. What seemed like flexible guidelines were immobilized by new European regulations; further, the company itself had moved on beyond making abrasives to a whole range of innovative products (think "Post-It"). Derided as "plumber's gothic," the 3M typeface did not suggest the high-tech company that 3M had become.[70]

In 1978, 3M's advertising agency, BBDO, recommended retaining Siegel & Gale to upgrade and simplify the corporate identity manual. After reviewing a cross section of materials 3M was using in the marketplace, Siegel told 3M that redoing its manual would merely be a Band-Aid fix. 3M's visual identity, he advised, required major surgery.

Over the ensuing six months Siegel and a team of designers met with 3M executives at the St. Paul, Minnesota, headquarters to conceptualize a new visual system to reflect the progressive, forward-looking culture of the company. The cornerstone of the program was a powerful but strikingly simple 3M logo, marrying the "3" and "M" in Helvetica bold typeface, printed in Mandarin red.

Steve Dunne, the younger brother of writers Dominic and John Gregory Dunne, produced a comprehensive design system incorporating a house typestyle, a color palette and design formats for all primary media (signage, trucks, brochures, advertising and packaging). In time, the Minnesota Mining and Manufacturing Company officially changed its name to 3M.[71]

3M, the client, enthusiastically supported the dynamic new program, perhaps, Siegel theorizes, because they "responded to its simplicity and directness," Midwestern traits that happened to resonate around the world. But senior executives as BBDO dismissed the new logo as too simple, too plain. "We successfully argued against adding any graphic gimmicks, such as slanting the 3 or the M," Siegel says. "This was my first experience dealing with people who shrunk away from simple, elegant solutions. It wouldn't be my last."[72]

Primal Voice

In retrospect, Siegel believes he first used the phrase "corporate voice" when he worked with 3M. "I thought of it as a metaphor for integrated communications," he said. "To me, that's when corporate identity morphed into corporate voice. I used the phrase to talk about the fusion of strategy, content and design to make a distinctive communications program that would enable companies to speak to the marketplace in a unique way.

"I was always a little ahead of the curve with positioning [a corporation], pushing the 'value' proposition, the messaging and the tone of 'voice.' It stemmed from my education and training, my legal background. I always felt that graphics are only part of the equation, and what we're trying to do is communicate with people. I eventually morphed 'corporate voice' into 'brand voice.' "[73]

Lacking formal training in design, Siegel nonetheless was well experienced in photography and art to understand the limitations of graphic symbols in communications. Marks without authentic referents are meaningless. Logos and graphic systems have to stand for something, have to represent an unassailable idea or a value system. Siegel & Gale created a full graphics system—typefaces, colors, grids and signature systems—to demonstrate how the new 3M logo would appear in all its public manifestations. It passed, almost with flying colors; a few executives opting for blue, the color of choice of perhaps eighty percent of all corporate logos, rather than the brazen red Siegel preferred. 3M was already using a blue logo, but contrary to his often-stated counsel to preserve built-up equity, Siegel persuaded the company to choose red in order to make a strong statement about change. Perhaps Siegel agreed with Emerson that "a foolish consistency is the hobgoblin of little minds."

During a long association with 3M, Siegel & Gale helped construct a global communications strategy to manage 3M's image worldwide, modernized its global corporate identity, brought clarity and consistency to all the company's communications, and created a global voice that speaks with a local accent.[74]

Underpinning the 3M identity is what Siegel & Gale

today calls the "brand promise." Says Charles Reisler, a former veteran executive at Siegel & Gale: "A company's brand is really an elusive thing. Brand encompasses the [company's] identity, experience, products, its people. 3M was innovation, broad shoulders, big tasks." With bold foresight, the company 3M "allowed employees ten percent of their time to experiment; new products were introduced in their people's spare time," Reisler says.[75]

Innovation, the consultants concluded, was the essence of 3M, the glue that bound its thousands of parts and the muscular corporation as well. Using huge photo decals (manufactured by 3M), Siegel & Gale plastered the company's 18-wheel trucks with "3M Innovation" superimposed over huge product photomontages, dramatically illustrating 3M's innovation in action.

Siegel & Gale's growth from a "logo and design company" to master brand builder was marked with major innovations of its own, in particular, the creation of Corporate Voice and Language Simplification. As with any new enterprise, the firm's progress was not a smooth upward curve. Clients departed from time to time, as did staff members. Infusions of capital, the lifeblood of growing businesses, were sought. At one point the subsidiary of a major U.S. bank, for which Siegel & Gale did considerable internal communications work, would not cough up the $90,000 it owed. The client phoned to demand its "deliverables," the strategic and graphic solutions Siegel & Gale produced for them. Siegel retorted: "You haven't paid me. I'm locking up the material in a safe and I'm going to Europe on a trip. Wire me the money or give me a certified check." Siegel got the money the next day.[76]

Even as a novice entrepreneur, Siegel realized that by staying nimble, open and aware, he could both keep ahead of the competition and closely guide his own business. "Many of our competitors did terrific work," he noted, "but went out of business because they didn't pay attention to negotiating fair contracts, billing their clients on time, collecting receivables and providing a capital structure to finance growth in down periods.

"It is also absolutely imperative to provide a stimulating work environment, give your employees an opportunity to take on more responsibility and feel free to make constructive suggestions on how to improve the firm, and be sure people get fair financial rewards when they deliver the goods."[77]

Chapter 5:

The Right to Understand

In 1975 I convinced First National City Bank (Citibank) to simplify its consumer loan agreement. How can the premier bank in the country ask consumers to sign and be bound by a completely unintelligible legal agreement that even their in-house lawyers couldn't read? In creating this project it was clear to me that this was a business. So I spent five years promoting plain English for business and government, selling this specialized service throughout the country, hiring and training a staff to handle incoming projects. At the same time I helped establish a graduate program at Carnegie Mellon University, to provide a laboratory for advancing the state of the art of Simplification and, incidentally, to train talented people to staff our highly specialized service. I also joined the faculty of Fordham University Law School to teach the first plain English writing course for lawyers.

—Alan Siegel[78]

Even in his youth, Siegel noticed how poorly written consumer instructions were in functional documents. His father once considered using Asian dye-transfer techniques as a side business to photoengraving. Reading the translated instructions accompanying the equipment his father received, Siegel eyed this startling sentence, "Address Honorable Red Knob." (Translation: "Turn the red knob.") The account of this youthful insight may be apocryphal or the germ for his long quest to make communication more precise and effective.[79]

Not long after joining Siegel & Gale, Don Ervin introduced Siegel to Dr. Rudolph Flesch. The Austrian-born psychologist and educator wrote the best-selling book *Why Johnny Can't Read*, published in 1955, which ignited the phonics revolution. Flesch championed the "readability" of a text with his proprietary Flesch Reading Scores, and was regarded as an avatar of clear communication. George Nelson, the brilliant designer for whom Ervin previously worked, employed Dr. Flesch to "simplify," in a schematic, color-coded way, new Social Security booklets, but Nelson never pursued simplification as a discrete business.[80]

After interviewing Dr. Flesch and reading his books, Siegel saw an opportunity to boost his firm's services to a higher level; to advance beyond merely redesigning materials to making them more accessible, functional and usable. Why, for example, should people accept, on blind faith, insurance policies they couldn't understand? And so when First National City Bank (later renamed Citibank) hired Siegel & Gale to update the bank's retail forms—signature cards, applications, loan agreements and customer correspondence materials—Siegel convinced the bank officials to allow him to simplify the language. Give it a shot, they said, but we're convinced the lawyers will object to your messing with the contract language.[81]

In 1974, Siegel hired Dr. Flesch to work with him to simplify Citibank's loan agreement form. Ervin designed the form, the first legal form based on the ideas of language simplification. It would become a watershed event in consumer protection and an early articulation of fulfilling Citibank's "brand promise" of being the nation's premier bank. Siegel later said:

> The impetus for plain English and simplicity was tied to what is now called customer relationship management—creating customer loyalty to the brand by aligning their behavior with their brand promise. So when the bank publicly stated they were committed to listening to and serving their customers, how could they make this claim if no one could read or understand the legal agreements they made customers sign? [82]

With the Vietnam War winding down and the Watergate debacle in the news, Siegel sensed a pervasive national distrust of "taking official language at face value." "There is a real need for clear and unambiguous language in a host of functional documents we use every day," he declared. "In social terms, people wanted a new right: the right to understand. They expressed a strong desire for clear regulations and forms from the public and private institutions they had grown to mistrust."[83]

Citibank was mainly interested in streamlining its loan form. Siegel, on the other hand, was offended by the form's abstruse language, technical terms and endless lists of remedies available to the bank. "In essence, Siegel and Flesch reorganized and rewrote the language to relate more closely to the way consumers think and act. While his marketing research and advertising background was helpful, it was his law school training that helped him cope with certain legal issues that had always been cited as obstacles to language simplification in legal forms," wrote Kenneth Morris, then president of Siegel & Gale.[84]

Morris, who has a PhD from Columbia University in the history of the English language and linguistics, joined Siegel & Gale in 1978 and subsequently headed Simplified Communications for years, leaving the firm in 1998. "What Alan accomplished was to transform the concept of plain language into a viable business," Morris says. "In the process, he promoted the business concept aggressively, making a name for himself, for the company, and for the idea of plain English."[85]

Reframing Forms

Citibank's installment loan note was one of the bank's most frequently used forms, and one of the more difficult for loan applicants to read, let alone understand. The larger-than-legal-sized document seemed unplanned. The main text was set in all caps, the line type sizes were plucked from five typestyles, and it was set in a 48.5-pica line (over eight inches long), with no leading between the paragraphs. Moreover, the text was set in a justified column (flush left, flush right) and printed in one color. The form presented an in-your-face wall of type.

The writing itself was a model of turgid legalese. For example, in the fine print, was this disclaimer:

(Before)

In the event of default in the payment of this or any other Obligation or the performance or observance of any term or covenant contained herein or in any note or other contract of agreement evidencing or relating to any Obligation or any Collateral on the Borrower's part to be performed or observed; or the undersigned Borrower shall die; or any of the undersigned become insolvent or make an assignment for the benefit of creditors; or a petition shall be filed by or against any of the undersigned under any provision of the Bankruptcy Act; or any money, securities or property of the undersigned now or hereafter on deposit with or in the possession or under the control of the Bank shall be attached or become subject to distraint proceedings or any order or process of any court; or the Bank shall deem itself to be insecure then and in any such event the Bank shall have the right (at its option), without demand or notice of any kind, to declare all or any part of the Obligations to be immediately due and payable, whereupon such Obligations shall become and be immediately due and payable, and the Bank shall have the right to exercise all the rights and remedies available to a secured party upon default under the Uniform Commercial Code (the "Code") in effect in New York at the time, and such other rights and remedies as may otherwise be provided by law.

This section, part of a longer paragraph, ran 244 words. In the new Citibank consumer loan note, Siegel & Gale replaced it with the following:

(After)

Default I'll be in default:
1. If I don't pay an installment on time; or
2. If any other creditor tries by legal process to take any money of mine in your possession.

This welcome brevity would not have been possible without the advice of Carl Felsenfeld, a Citicorp vice president and chief legal counsel for the company's consumer-related operations. "Perhaps our hardest task was not writing things in English," Felsenfeld said, "but rather identifying clauses taken from traditional (commercial) contracts that could be eliminated without basic injury to the validity and legal enforceability of our consumer documents. Here, we were able to draw upon business experience and analyze contractual provisions that really had been used, as contrasted with those that provided protections recommended by lawyers largely for other contexts."[86]

At age 79, Felsenfeld today is 22 years into his second

career as professor of law at The Fordham University Law School in New York City, teaching banking law. Recalling his collaboration with Siegel, whom he characterizes as "smart, able and very aware of newfound opportunities," Felsenfeld believes the restructured loan agreement provided Citibank sufficient legal protection, and has stood the test of time. The document broke new ground, but Felsenfeld acknowledges that some recidivism is to be expected, given the waves of succeeding generations of lawyers charged with dealing with consumer lawsuits. "Ultimately, the documents get into the hands of lawyers," he says. "What is needed is some leeway that gives contract draftsmen the ability to generalize, versus particularizing; we need a sense of freedom." In the 1970s, Felsenfeld introduced Siegel to the dean of Fordham Law. Siegel proposed a course titled "Writing Contracts in Plain English," and taught the first plain English writing course for law students for four years. With Felsenfeld, Siegel co-authored *Simplified Consumer Credit Forms* (Wodham, Gorham and LaMont, 1978) and *Writing Contracts in Plain English* (West Publishing, 1981).[87]

With little to guide him except his own business acumen, Siegel examined the Citibank loan agreement with fresh eyes. "Our focus was on using our communications, writing and design skills to create a consumer contract that consumers and bank employees could read and understand, at the same time sending a strong signal that this was not your typical legal document," Siegel said.[88]

Drawing on their collective common sense and experience, Siegel & Gale reorganized the loan form to display information in a sequence that was meaningful to the consumer. They personalized the text, substituting "I", "we", "your" and other pronouns for such off-putting phrases as "undersigned Borrower(s)" and "Bank." Instead of cumbersome locutions like "For value received, the undersigned (jointly and severally) hereby promise(s) to pay . . . ," they simply wrote: "To repay my loan, I promise to pay you. . . ." They shortened sentence length by using contractions and the active, instead of passive, voice, which also aided clarity. They divided the note into subsections highlighted with boldface headlines, which improved readability measurably. New material not required by law was added, Siegel wrote, "to make the document informative as well as legally binding," such as the clause ". . . if this loan is refinanced—that is, replaced by another note—you will . . ." ("Refinanced" wasn't even explained in the original version.)[89]

Reorganizing the document's appearance, Siegel & Gale divided the page into a five-column grid. Two type sizes in one style—Times Roman upper- and lowercase—were used in two weights. The line length was reduced to 37 picas (six inches long). The text was set flush left and ragged right, and printed in two colors. The result was an effective format, eminently readable and strikingly simple in appearance. The restructuring demonstrated that simplifying and redesigning printed texts are inseparable. Moreover, the Simplification team won the support of the two senior-most consumer credit lawyers at the bank, Felsenfeld and Duncan McDonald. Without their backing—they effectively neutralized internal criticism—the document would have been dismantled by other bank lawyers.

As the Simplification practice matured, Siegel & Gale devised a methodology to test consumers reading plain English documents, then performing certain tasks as directed by the documents or answering questions. Document effectiveness was measured by the accuracy of responses, the time taken to complete a task and interpretation of verbatim participant reactions. Siegel & Gale's confidence in the clarity of the information it presented was borne out by exploring and testing alternatives with users, and making adjustments guided by their responses.[90]

Designed to Communicate

Siegel & Gale's designers and language simplifiers knew they needed to experiment to make legal forms not just more understandable but also more appealing. "The typical designer who gets a degree from one of the art-oriented schools won't want to design forms," Siegel said at the time. "You not only have to understand the elements of design and be able to work within very severe restrictions, you also must, to a degree, be well-read, literate and able to work with people in law, psychology and linguistics—areas with which many designers are not comfortable."[91]

The firm employed a zero-based approach to simplification projects. As there was little precedent to draw from, no linguistic dogma to guide him and a slim bank of talent to tap, Siegel asked what, realistically, had to go into a document and why. His marketing and advertising experience dealt with consumer behavior, and his law school training prepared him to deal with legal concepts and language. Legal barriers that at first seemed insurmountable became malleable under closer study.

Siegel framed his approach as real-world problem solving. "If you send simplified language to a typical forms printer," he said, "they will produce a traditional form. It will be difficult to read because of the layout and typography, and its appearance will turn people off." He rallied his designers to think in terms of structure, appearance and readability, the basic premises of good design, and they delivered.

"The designer also has to love type," remarks former Siegel & Gale senior designer Ann Breaznell, a Skidmore graduate who received an MFA in graphic design and typography at Yale and taught there. She sought typographical strengths in selecting designers. Her staff became increasingly involved in the writing and rewriting of the documents. Siegel believed that designers required much more than graphics skills, because "they have to . . . respond to research, challenge lawyers on language and continually push clients in new design directions."[92] In this respect, Siegel & Gale helped elevate design from illustration to a high level of clear and accurate information presentation, an idea that may not sound novel today but was prescient 30 years ago.

Preaching Plain English

For Language Simplification to become a viable business, it needed wider public exposure and intrepid clients. Fortunately, Siegel understood the power of credible publicity. He wanted to make the case that document simplification builds customer loyalty and employee morale and can save money. Equally important, it was the right thing to do in an open society. With the advice of Richard Weiner, who left Ruder & Finn to start his own public relations company, Siegel launched a publicity blitz to promote the merits of language simplification.

The media coverage was enormous. Local New York radio and television shows, the Los Angeles *Times*, Washington *Star*, *The New York Times*, and all the major business and trade publications covered the redesigned Citibank loan note. *The New York Times*, in a Feb. 4, 1978, piece about New York State Assemblyman Peter M. Sullivan's consumer protection initiative, alluded to Siegel as "the country's leading consultant on business language simplification." Siegel was interviewed on NBC's *Today Show* by consumer reporter Betty Furness and participated in a debate on plain English on PBS's *MacNeil/Lehrer Report*. Dan Rather, on the CBS Evening News, cited the firm's work. *People* magazine ran a three-page Q & A titled "Wherein the Party of the First Part, Expert Alan Siegel, Wants to Ban Contract Legalese." Weiner recently recalled: "Alan was a terrific interviewee; tall, good-looking, full of energy and enthusiasm," adding that Siegel had become somewhat of a "celebrity—he's had that and still has that."[93]

Key opinion-shapers endorsed the project. Consumer advocate Ralph Nader commented favorably on Siegel's efforts, as did NBC's Edwin Newman, who regularly wrote and broadcast on English and the language arts. Arguably, no one was more important than Bess Meyerson, Citibank's head of consumer affairs. The program would not have seen the light of day, Siegel says, had she not effectively convinced Citibank President William Spencer on its benefits.[94]

Siegel's timing was exquisite. Consumerism, at last backed by legislative teeth, was sweeping the nation. Awareness of the need for clear language in transactional documents was growing. New York State Assemblyman Peter M. Sullivan wrote the country's first Plain English law in 1977, requiring that contracts of $50,000 or less primarily for personal, family or household purposes must be written in clear and coherent language with everyday meanings.[95] To date, more than forty states have adopted laws requiring contracts to be written in clear and readable English.

The U.S. government has a long, cyclical interest in creating documents that are clear in meaning. After World War II, an employee of the Bureau of Land Management wrote a book called *Gobbledygook Has Gotta Go*.[96] It didn't. In the 1970s, President Nixon gave plain language a boost by ordering the Federal Register be written in "layman's terms." President Carter, in 1978, issued an executive order mandating that government regulations be made "cost-effective and easy to understand"; it was rescinded by President Reagan. President Clinton attempted to revive the plain language movement in government and assigned Vice President Al Gore to encourage its use, with minor success. Several government agencies, most conspicuously the Federal Aviation Administration, require clearly written communications and have issued guidelines to that end. To date, George W. Bush's administration has no formal plain language initiative.[97]

The Document Design Project

Perhaps the most significant government contribution to language simplification was the Document Design Project (1978–1981), funded by the Department of Education. It was an exhaustive study of public documents to help willing federal agencies communicate in plain language. The contract was awarded to a tripartite team: the not-for-profit American Institutes for Research (AIR), Carnegie-Mellon University and Siegel & Gale. The consortium assisted agencies in drafting plain language regulations and documents, such as the Housing & Urban Development rules for the Privacy Act and clearer forms for students applying for financial assistance. One of the project's publications, *Guidelines for Document Designers*, done in 1980 on a typewriter, is still used by government writers.[98]

The Document Design group conducted original research on government programs and prepared a definitive study of all research relating to the simplification of government and legal communications. Siegel served on the executive committee that ran the project, supervised some original research and worked directly with the other partner organizations.[99] The project uniquely integrated theory and research with practice. Its purpose was not to "correct" documents, but to find creative solutions to writing comprehensible and persuasive texts. Organization and document format were deemed as important as language choices.

The overall impact of the Document Design Project remains positive. Says Janice Redish, the project's former director: "It had a tremendous influence at that time, and has an ongoing influence. There is a lot from what Alan, our colleagues and I were doing that has become part of ordinary expectations." She credits lawyer Felsenfeld for taking prudent risks with the Citibank loan note; that is, eliminating protective legal clauses needed only rarely, in the service of better communication. Redish, who earned a PhD in linguistics from Harvard, has been at the forefront of clear communications, a pioneer in testing computer software usage and in online document design.[100]

Siegel's role in promoting the Plain Language movement was seminal. He worked closely with Carnegie Mellon University, which was awarded a grant from the National Institutes for Education to create two graduate programs, the master of arts in professional writing (in contrast to "creative writing") and a PhD in rhetoric.[101] Siegel co-founded and was co-director of the Communications Design Center at Carnegie Mellon for a number of years, and taught there as an associate professor.

Says Siegel: "I spent considerable time in Pittsburgh working with the head of the Psychology Department and Professor Erwin Steinberg, who was the original dean of the Humanities School and a James Joyce scholar. In his free time he taught plain English writing to businessmen, and we mobilized specialists in statistics, rhetoric, graphic design, cognitive psychology and computer science to create the Communications Design Center."[102]

Now in his 60th year at Carnegie Mellon, Dr. Steinberg teaches a course in style for the Master's in Professional Writing program. Still using the "beautifully done brochure" titled *Simple Is Smart*, which was created 25 years ago by Siegel & Gale, he contends that plain English and Simplified Communications are one and the same. Says Dr. Steinberg: "Alan gives clients a voice and a face, and language is part of the voice."[103]

Simplification's Legacy

A major dividend of Siegel's association with Carnegie Mellon is the university's graduates: over the years more than 50 have contributed greatly to the success of Siegel & Gale. One of the most brilliant is Irene Etzkorn. She applied for Carnegie Mellon's MA in professional writing, in the new program's first class. Previously, she worked as a tax examiner at the cavernous Holtsville, Long Island, IRS processing center, and also was a census-taker. "I was shocked at people filing their tax returns in crayons," she says. "It was so obvious that people had no clue as to what they were doing," a condition she found repeatedly in taking the census.[104]

In her first semester at Carnegie Mellon, Etzkorn heard Siegel give a guest lecture about his firm's language projects, and discovered a company attempting to rectify real, not theoretical, communications problems. "You could feel that he believed it," she says. He presented case studies of how his firm was simplifying communications for banks, insurance companies, the IRS and the Census Bureau. Siegel's lecture sealed her career choice.[105]

Grasping "how important Siegel & Gale's work could be," she plunged into the interdisciplinary program, a curriculum that included such practical skills as technical writing, professional writing and computer programming, along with theory-based courses such as modern rhetorical theory and cognitive science. "Alan's charismatic delivery, the glamour of a midtown Manhattan office and his recent profile in *People* magazine were all it took for me to know where I wanted to work," she says.[106]

Etzkorn began as a summer intern at Siegel & Gale in 1981 and went on to work on the firm's most challenging simplification projects, including creating new federal income tax forms. She ultimately rose to head of the Simplified Communications Group and, now in a consulting capacity, continues to break new ground in simplification work for major corporations and government units.

Watershed Projects

These examples of Siegel & Gale's watershed projects are a sampling of those that buoyed Simplification to new levels, in terms of business impact and innovative communications:[107]

CITIBANK LOAN NOTE: The seminal Simplification project, done relatively quickly, elicited positive consumer reaction and publicity, leading to broader projects.

CENSUS FORM: The first census form that people completed themselves rather than answer a census-taker's questions.

FEDERAL TAX FORMS SIMPLIFICATION: In a three-year project, Siegel & Gale, together with the accounting company Deloitte Haskins and Sells, research firm Yankelovich, Skelly & White, and a readability expert, formulated new thinking on improving accuracy of calculations by using algorithms; customized forms by filing status; introduced examples and work charts; simplified terminology; and applied structuring, packaging and other simplification techniques. The test results were outstanding, but the government cherry-picked solutions, notably the addition of Form 1040EZ and the radically redesigned instructional packages.[108]

CHUBB MASTERPIECE POLICY: The first completely simplified insurance product. Modular and printed on demand, the package comprised an insurance policy, premium statements, renewals, notices, auto insurance card and a rating system used by agents, resulting in a distinctive product brand.

SHEARSON-LEHMAN BROKERAGE STATEMENT: The first truly readable brokerage statement in the industry, and one that became widely emulated. Many features are taken for granted today, such as a summary page showing types of investments, change in value, percentage of portfolio, earnings to date, and capital gains and losses. Shearson underwent a succession of ownership changes, but after 20 years the pioneering statement remains fresh and familiar.

GTE TELEPHONE BILL: Siegel & Gale's first simplified phone bill was done for NYNEX, but its GTE bill was far more complex, featuring the first one-to-one marketing messages to promote customer calling plans based on usage patterns. Though both companies were merged out of existence, the simplified bills are widely emulated.

AMP (AUSTRALIA) FORMS SYSTEM: Siegel & Gale demonstrated how to standardize a wide range of insurance forms by creating templates for a laser printer that served as a "filter" for all the forms.

WSJ FINANCIAL GUIDES: Beginning in 1989, Siegel and Kenneth Morris collaborated in producing a series of financial guides. All but the first book, *The Wall Street Journal Guide to Understanding Money & Markets*, written with Richard Wurman and issued by Access Press, were published by Lightbulb Press, jointly owned by Siegel and Morris. The books were based on the principles of language simplification and distributed widely by *The Wall Street Journal*, their main underwriter, selling more than two million copies nationwide. Copiously illustrated, written in plain English and handsomely printed, the 5″ by 10″ paperback books demystified financial subjects from personal finance and taxes to investing and retirement.

Siegel believes the guides have been useful for journalists, MBA students and consumers: "When I do interviews on cable business shows, journalists tell me they used the guides to become familiar with business terms when they started their careers. I see the books in client offices across the country."[109]

"The impact of simplification in document creation is so profound we now take it for granted," says Ann Breaznell, who teaches typography at the College of St. Rose. "Now you're so used to looking at materials that have already gone through this process that it's very hard to imagine how bad and how complicated documents were." Only when one compares the documents before and after they were simplified does the change seem dramatic. Siegel, she says, "has a way of seeing things that other people don't."[110] Etzkorn agrees: "Alan is one of the founding fathers of the plain English movement."[111] Of Siegel's many achievements, his wife, Gloria, is especially proud "of the early language work he did for Citibank and the IRS. There would be a public outcry if people realized he simplified the U.S. income forms, which were largely discarded by the Reagan administration when Carter was voted out of office."[112]

Chapter 6:

Defining Corporate Voice

The vast majority of corporations, not-for-profits and government agencies present muddled communications to their employees, customers and other constituents. Corporations simply haven't developed a distinctive, powerful language to define who they are, what they do and what they stand for—a distinctive corporate voice. . . . To communicate effectively and build a distinctive identity, an organization must develop its own voice—a voice that is instantly recognizable, a voice that conjures up strong images and associations, a voice that fuses content, language and design to communicate the organization's distinctive personality, vision and point of view. With a unified corporate voice, every facet of a organization's communications can build on its identity, leveraging communications opportunities across all media with consistent, focused messages . . . finding this voice, designing and managing it, is one of the most critical and complex issues facing corporate management.

—Alan Siegel[13]

Siegel & Gale's list of clients grew impressively in the 1980s and 1990s, the lessons learned from each project increasing the firm's knowledge base and capabilities. The firm described itself as an international communications consultancy, with major offices in New York, London and Los Angeles, and a handful of satellite affiliates scattered throughout the globe, depending on where new business was being generated.

Voice Lessons

Siegel moved decisively toward modern branding practice when he began refining and codifying the firm's integrated corporate communications programs under the rubric of Corporate Voice. Siegel wrote that, in the 1980s, his company "challenged conventional communications practices" by transforming corporate identity into Corporate Voice programs. The goal of Corporate Voice, he said, was to "define a company's unique business proposition and see to it that the company uses every point of contact with its customers to speak in one consistent, focused and unique voice." In helping other companies find their voices, both Alan Siegel and his firm were to find their own voice as well.[114]

In an extended tutorial for new employees in 1994, Kenneth Cooke, Siegel & Gale's creative director, drew sharp distinctions between identity and voice: "We're involved in conceptual art rather than in graphics execution. Our footprint is our deliverable: we conceive, design and produce Corporate Voice. We are all working to a single ideal, an overarching strategy, and we can implement solutions at a high level."[115]

The "overarching strategy" is realized through a holistic approach to corporate communications—the cross-disciplined orchestration of branding, naming, advertising, corporate identity, simplified communications, interactive media and design. "Identity," Cooke said, "has to work in concert with everything a company does and says. It's the totality of expression." Corporate Voice, he emphasized, "is *not* a mechanism to sell all our services. We want messages working together to *resonate*."

Siegel & Gale's method was to *define* the components of Corporate Voice, *test* the findings and finally to *execute* the Voice. Lacking in-house research capability, Siegel & Gale contracted out assignments to independent firms like Yankelovich, Skelly & White. Siegel welcomed the detachment of outside research experts, strongly believing his firm could jeopardize its credibility were it even to appear to assess its own work.

He advanced a psychological model as the basis for Corporate Voice analysis:[116] The corporation's *personality attributes* are elicited from interviews (often done by Siegel) with management, employees, other corporate constituencies and a great deal of independent homework.[117] The project team probes for the company's heritage, culture, resources, vision, values and specific differences in relation to its industry and competition. Based on the data captured, the Siegel & Gale team crafts a *positioning statement*, which defines the "big idea" or a single-minded proposition that succinctly distills the organization's essence. Crucially, the positioning must be *supported by facts*. Siegel demands that all positioning statements be *unique, differentiate* the client from the competition and be rendered in *distinctive language.* The acid test is that the positioning must be *credible, clear* and *relevant.* The team then constructs a *strategy* to express the positioning, suggesting appropriate messages, graphics, imagery and language, as well as the media for expression: advertising, public relations, stationery systems, employee information, down to how telephone calls should be answered.

Often the staples of corporate identity makeovers hinge on making a new logo (a symbolic gesture), slogan or an "image" campaign. In contrast, Corporate Voice aims to create a *distinctive, long-term cohesive and comprehensive communications platform*—one that can be tested before execution to ensure that it motivates supportive behavior. Siegel refers to this as the "so what?" factor, as in "so what can your program do for me, the client?"[118]

Distinctive Voices

Siegel places a high premium on the proposition that "to cut through the noise of the marketplace, a corporation must speak with a clear, coherent and distinctive voice."[119]

In a speech to the Conference Board, he adduced the analogy of the writer's voice, the perceived sense of the person behind the prose, poetry or drama. "Most people can describe the voice of a favorite author," he said. "Ernest Hemingway's distinctive mode of expression, for instance, was spare and selective, easily parodied because it was so readily identifiable."[120]

The speech, and countless others like it, was based on an elegant booklet written by Siegel & Gale, titled *Corporate Voice: A New Approach to Communications in the 1990s*. With striking visuals and language inspired by thoughtful analysis, the booklet was produced by Crane Business Papers, which had invited Siegel to speak before a gathering of respected business communicators. There, Siegel distilled these corporate voices of companies familiar to most audiences:[121]

Apple Computer's voice is brash, exuberant and irreverent. It celebrates a new generation and a new way of thinking, in which the individual—not the boss, the company or other authority—reigns supreme. Its evocative symbol, witty, informative and irreverent writing style, airy and sophisticated graphics, and its imaginative advertising and product design—even down to the whimsical icons on its computer screens—all lend support to this powerful message. This truly "corporate" voice can be as crystal clear as an individual's. It speaks for all the people who work for a company, buy its products or identify with its values.

Ralph Lauren. To look at a Ralph Lauren ad or even to walk into [his] shop is to enter a complete fantasy world, sprung full-blown from one man's imagination. Lauren's blockbuster ads feature page after page of men's and women's fashions, home furnishings, luggage, shoes, accessories and other merchandise—together with fairy-tale settings, gorgeous models with fine, aristocratic features, and fantastic, striking props. It all adds up to a seamless environment—so convincing you can visualize these people's lives and take away a realistic idea of who they are, where they went to school, where they shop and what they do behind closed doors. . . . The products almost seem secondary to the fully realized settings and fully imagined lives. . . . The ultimate source of [the company's] distinctive voice is within Lauren himself. . . . "For me to put my name on anything," Lauren has said, "I have to want to own it."

Tiffany & Co. Though it has all the opulence and luxury associated with [other] exclusive jewelers, the name "Tiffany & Co." carries a special magic that enables it to appeal to a far broader audience. Tiffany's voice is accessible elegance—exclusive without being elitist, glamorous without being intimidating. For the mass of ordinary Americans who can't afford to shop there regularly, a gift from Tiffany is something special. You can't go wrong if your gift arrives in that celebrated blue box.

Metropolitan Life. In an industry not known for verve and excitement, Metropolitan Life always stood among the most traditional. . . . But when it went public with a new ad campaign in 1985, it uncharacteristically chose the Peanuts comic strip characters as its new corporate "spokesgang." Snoopy, Charlie Brown, Lucy, Woodstock—it's hard to imagine a less likely voice for conservative Met Life. Cheerful and lighthearted, this new voice forms an unexpected yet endearing counterpoint to a usually somber industry. . . . The vigor and consistency of its voice make the company stand out against faceless competitors . . . a welcome touch of personality to a business that rarely shows one.

Like the DNA of a living organism, Siegel's "voiceprint" analyses of these companies is so on point, they could have been written last week. In fact, the booklet was printed in 1989. In spreading the word of his Voice gospel, Siegel reinforced his thesis by describing the unique characteristics of other strong corporate voices—Walt Disney, The Gap, Braun and Herman Miller. The voices rang true to his audiences, and invariably he won them over. With periodic recalibrations, all the voices have endured to this day, a tribute to their careful stewardship and execution.

Successful voice programs are characterized by *consistency, clarity* and *credibility,* Siegel often repeated in mantra-like fashion to prospects, clients and associates alike. Extending his "author's voice" metaphor, a writer doesn't whimsically alternate between first person and third person, or suddenly inject formality where a tone of intimacy was clearly established. To the reader, such jarring switches are confusing and off-putting.

Modern theorists trace the basis for reputation management as far back as Aristotle's rhetorical appeals: *logos*, *pathos* and *ethos*. *Logos* relies on reason, the plausibility of evidence to buttress a position. *Pathos* works on one's emotions. And *ethos* asks the critical question: can you trust this voice?[122] Put another way: is the voice consistent; is it transparent; is it credible; does the receiver understand and *want* to believe the message and the messenger? All three appeals, in varying measures, drive Corporate Voice. Done well, Voice addresses the authenticity, believability and character of the rhetorician (the company); importantly, Voice can shape audience perceptions of the corporate speaker.

Engineering the Voice Model

The idea of Corporate Voice, invoked early by Siegel but used sporadically at first, was not born whole. The inchoate elements that coalesced into the Voice program emerged from more than a decade of challenging assignments; improvements in design capabilities, diagnostic research, name generation and nomenclature systems; the introduction of new technologies; and careful cultivation of client relationships.

Among the projects and new capabilities that added content, direction and timbre to Corporate Voice, and to Brand Voice as well, these should be noted:

Chubb. In 1984, The Chubb Group of Insurance Companies initially wanted a simplified personal insurance policy to cover the unique needs of its high-net-worth clients. Research found Chubb's process of issuing insurance "cumbersome, time consuming, costly and extremely confusing . . ."[123] The Siegel & Gale team developed a policy system to protect art collections, luxury cars and houses, and aptly named it Masterpiece®. Using electronic technology and documents written in personal language, they streamlined Chubb's underwriting process to accommodate individuals and families. The program was built on a brand value proposition reflecting Chubb's financial strength, sophisticated loss-control consulting and a "customer first" approach to claims handling. As the program was extended to other insurance lines, the firm helped shape and communicate Chubb's distinctive voice through an array of media, especially the elegant advertising created by Larry Oakner, a radio advertising writer, and Peter Swerdloff, then a copywriter, now senior strategist of Siegel & Gale. "Chubb's voice is always elegant, sophisticated and understated," Siegel said.[124] During a 15-year relationship with Siegel & Gale, Chubb benefited from striking gains in its familiarity, secured a dominant market share in the high-net-worth personal lines market, and enjoyed recognition for giving good customer value by settling claims quickly and fairly.

Xerox's image fell to an all-time low in the mid-1980s. Its name became synonymous in a generic way with making photocopies. The widespread misperception that Xerox was just a "copier company" could hamper further expansion into other areas of the office market. In reality, Xerox already was moving into electronic printing and publishing, carving out a unique niche in document management. In positioning Xerox as "The Document Company," Siegel & Gale shifted the marketing focus to the output of Xerox's machines from the machines themselves.[125] Laser-sharp, the positioning helped alleviate Xerox's identity problems, illuminated a clear vision for the future and served as a platform for launching production publishing products.[126]

Caterpillar. The world's largest manufacturer of construction and mining equipment, Caterpillar decentralized its structure in 1990, bringing it closer to its markets, but inadvertently freeing aggressive profit centers to modify their trademarks into a nominal goulash. Siegel persuaded management that Caterpillar's identity was "more than a logo and graphics . . . It was intimately tied to values and a sense of the company's mission."[127] The new positioning was: "Caterpillar enables the world's planners and builders to turn their ideas into realities. It's not only what we make that makes us proud—it's what we make possible." Company communicators trained at Siegel & Gale work-shops engaged employees worldwide in the "One Voice" program, as Caterpillar called it. One Voice resounded in ads in major business news outlets and on sports and news programs. TV and print ads showed Caterpillar's equipment tearing down the Berlin Wall and extinguishing blazing oil wells in Kuwait. The decadelong program, featuring TV and print ads created by Peter Swerdloff, empow-ered Caterpillar with a more disciplined approach to cultivating its voice (i.e., brand, at this point) and demonstrated the indispensability of employee education to drive home the brand's value.

Memorable Design

Perhaps because Siegel contextualizes—some might say subjugates—logos and graphic design in his pursuit of the ultimate goal, which is to make winning brands, his firm is not fairly credited for its design capabilities. In fact, Siegel & Gale's design portfolio has from the start glittered with uniquely communicative logotypes and visual styles appropriate to their clients' personalities.

The *Mellon* bank mark holds up well after three decades, even though Mellon's three encircled hash marks were perceived by management as an "m," while the designer merely intended a reference to the bank's three major business lines.[128]

Acura's "A" marque, the work of Jim Cross, a former Siegel & Gale designer and partner, is recognized worldwide as a craftsman's calipers, the symbol of Acura's "Precision-Crafted Performance." (In Japan the logo could conceivably be read as a variation on the venerated Shinto Torii, or temple gate, used by Acura's parent company, Honda.)

Nortel's "globe mark," an iconic armillary replacing the "o" in Nortel, graphically illustrates its positioning, "A World of Networks."

New York City's *MTA* (Metropolitan Transit Authority) logo, an initialed circle that visually recedes into a train tunnel, symbolically integrates formerly disparate systems, all tunnel users, into the world's largest regional transportation network.

Dell's logo, with the "E" standing on edge, just as the company stood the PC industry on its ear, is one of Siegel & Gale's most memorable designs.

More recently, the firm created the *Blue* holograph credit card from *American Express*, with an embedded "smart chip"—"a dramatic departure from the conservative green American Express cards," *I.D.* magazine wrote.[129]

All are handsome, simple, sometimes minimalist designs, freighted with meaning and long-lived.

Howard Belk, Co-Managing Director of the New York office, has been in the job for the last three years. But, in fact, he met Siegel when he was 22 years old, some 25 years ago, when Belk was working as a freelance designer at night in Siegel & Gale's offices in New York's Stevens Building. Siegel happened to enter a semi-dark room, saw Belk and thundered: "Who the hell are you?" Today, Siegel recognizes Belk not only as New York's co-managing director but also the head of Design, a role in which Belk is intimately involved in concept development. Acknowledging that the "centrifugal force at Siegel & Gale is strategy—powerful and simple," Belk says: "We want to able to leverage new technology and help organizations uniquely to bring the brand into the customer relationship. That's our core business in a world that's changing fast: smart language, a voice and aftercare. We have no house design style; freshness of ideas counts."[130]

Belk recounts a meeting that he, Siegel and other colleagues had with former senator Bob Kerrey. Kerrey is now the president of The New School, an urban university whose very existence defies academic conventions. (See "Breakthough Brands," Chapter 9.) Reviewing preliminary designs with Senator Kerrey and his advisors, Siegel said (according to Belk): "We have a design that breaks all the rules, but when we get to it, you probably won't like it." "That [challenge] was all it took," recalls Belk. "Kerrey chose it, we refined it, and it is the one in use today."

Photographs and Illustrations

Siegel attracted considerable attention for his basketball prowess at
Long Beach High School on Long Island in 1955 and 1956, when he was
selected by *Dell* magazine as one of the top players in the country.

In September 1956, Siegel
matriculated at Cornell
University in Ithaca, New
York. He graduated from
the School of Industrial
and Labor Relations in-
tent on becoming a labor
lawyer.

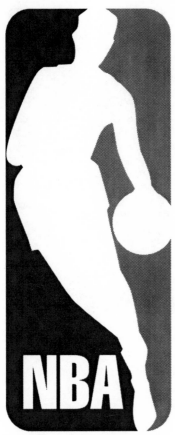

Uniroyal, formerly known as US Rubber, was Siegel & Gale's first major identity program. The trademark was derived from the tire mark used on its retail outlets.

The NBA's ubiquitous logo and corporate identity was based on a photograph of basketball legend Jerry West from *Sport* magazine.

Siegel & Gale was hired in 1975 to create the new identity for The Consolidated Rail Corporation (CONRAIL)— the entity formed to replace six bankrupt railroads in the Northeast. The graphic representation was based on the chairman's statement that a railroad is "steel wheels on steel rails."

Pitney Bowes

A logo with legs, the 1971 Pitney Bowes logo is a cruciform of nesting right angles, symbolizing the precise repetition of the postage meter and the company's continuing technological innovation.

Alan Siegel raised the visibility and benefits of simplified legal, medical, and government communications in speeches, articles, and testimony before congressional committees. His presentations were reprinted and distributed widely.

In 1977, 3M introduced a powerful new logo and a global voice program that spoke with a local accent to bring clarity and consistency to their communications.

Siegel & Gale worked with the Interbank Card Association to rename Master Charge to MasterCard and create a new global identity.

Mellon Bank worked with Alan Siegel in 1981 to reposition the bank from a regional bank into a major national bank. The stylized "M" trademark boldly identifies Mellon at a glance and is still in use today.

The power of plain English, promoted widely by Alan Siegel, made national news in the 1970s and 1980s with Siegel appearing on the *MacNeil/Lehrer Report, The Today Show,* and the *CBS Evening News;* in interviews in *The New York Times, Los Angeles Times,* and a striking spread in *People* magazine.

Default I'll be in default:
1. If I don't pay an installment on time; or
2. If any other creditor tries by legal process to take any money of mine in your possession.

You can then demand immediate payment of the balance of this note, minus the part of the finance charge which hasn't been earned figured by the rule of 78. You will also have other legal rights, for instance, the right to repossess, sell and apply security to the payments under this note and any other debts I may then owe you.

The seminal simplification project: Siegel & Gale's popular, easy-to-read loan note for First National City Bank (now Citibank) supplanted an impenetrable document. The concise, new default section (I'll be in default if I don't pay an installment on time) replaced a 287-word paragraph that attempted to spell out every kind of default.

The self administered census form (in contrast to answering a census-taker's questions) is another "first" developed by Siegel & Gale's Simplification team for testing in the 1980 census.

During the Carter administration in the late 1970s, Siegel & Gale was retained by the IRS to simplify individual taxpayer instructions and forms. The current EZ form, which helped ease the burden of filing for millions of taxpayers, grew out of this work.

Siegel & Gale helped Chubb build a powerful voice and a penetrating marketing program in the personal property casualty business by creating Masterpiece, a comprehensive policy covering all the needs of upscale customers in one plain English policy. The product and the company were positioned around the theme "We cost more, but we're worth it."

The new graphic identity Siegel & Gale created for Dell in 1992 embodies the company's irrepressible spirit that stood the PC industry on its ear by selling directly to the customer.

XEROX
THE
DOCUMENT
COMPANY

Positioning Xerox at the forefront of document management helped the company move beyond its limiting identity of a copier company and carve out a unique niche that embraced its innovative, electronic printing and publishing capabilities.

The Wall Street Journal Guides, created by Alan Siegel and Kenneth Morris, demystify and simplify subjects from personal finance and taxes to investing and retirement. Through clear writing and user-friendly information design, these books were on numerous bestseller lists for a decade.

Siegel & Gale has completed over 200 card design projects for American Express during the past eight years. The Blue Card is American Express's first transparent card, artfully designed and featuring an embedded electronic chip and blue hologram.

ⳑ NOVARTIS

In 1996, Sandoz and arch rival, Swiss-based, pharmaceutical giant Ciba-Geigy merged. Siegel & Gale developed the Novartis name—from the Latin "new skills"—and positioned the company as "The world's leading life sciences company."

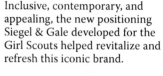

Living.
Improved daily.

Inclusive, contemporary, and appealing, the new positioning Siegel & Gale developed for the Girl Scouts helped revitalize and refresh this iconic brand.

Siegel & Gale repositioned Dow in 2000 from a commodities manufacturer to a consumer essentials company.

The Metropolitan Transportation Authority (MTA) operates the largest and most complex regional transportation system in the United States. A unifying identity system embracing subways, buses, commuter trains, and bridges was needed to facilitate employment of the MetroCard, an electronic payment card that replaced tokens, transfers, and exact change.

BOISE

Berklee
college *of*
music
Nothing Conservatory About It

SunTrust

Diversification beyond paper making inspired Siegel & Gale to advise
Boise Cascade to drop "Cascade" and its emblematic tree, simplify its
brand architecture, and build messages around the positioning: Work.
Build. Create.

The new positioning for Lehman Brothers "Where Vision Gets Built,"
was based on this leading investment banking firm's history of funding
industrial innovation. It has effectively served as a unifying force for the
brand and the firm.

Siegel & Gale worked with the Berklee College of Music, the world's
largest, independent music college, to raise their profile around edgy
positioning: Nothing Conservatory About It.

In 2004, Siegel & Gale created a new visual identity to
re-launch the SunTrust brand after a series of mergers in over 1,500 retail
branches, the Internet, and events and marketing communications.

THE NEW SCHOOL

THE NEW SCHOOL FOR GENERAL STUDIES

THE NEW SCHOOL FOR SOCIAL RESEARCH

MILANO THE NEW SCHOOL FOR MANAGEMENT AND URBAN POLICY

PARSONS THE NEW SCHOOL FOR DESIGN

EUGENE LANG COLLEGE THE NEW SCHOOL FOR LIBERAL ARTS

MANNES COLLEGE THE NEW SCHOOL FOR MUSIC

THE NEW SCHOOL FOR DRAMA

THE NEW SCHOOL FOR JAZZ AND CONTEMPORARY MUSIC

Siegel & Gale helped The New School, the unconventional, eclectic, and
activist university in Greenwich Village, integrate eight highly independent
colleges with an overarching university identity.

Chapter 7:
What's *Really* in a Name

A Short History of Modern Naming: Since the 1800s, most businesses in America were named for their founders. Between World I and the mid-twentieth century, companies tried to project "dominance" with descriptive names on horizontal industrial buildings (General Motors, et al). When these proved unreadable on office towers and products, a corporate Esperanto of initials and acronyms evolved. Made-up names, frequently with no apparent meaning, spread into global markets, e.g., Sony and Kodak. Countless names were spawned by deregulation of telecommunications and other industries, mergers and acquisitions, and the dot-com boom. The appetite for trendy, off-beat names on the Internet remains insatiable.[131]

One of the most challenging tasks for brand consultants is developing corporate and brand names. Organizations require new names when they merge, divest business units, consolidate a number of business units, and create new products and services. An increasing number of joint ventures require their own brand identity. As companies stretch to reach global markets, they continually must evaluate how to build a unified brand identity that works in a multitude of languages and cultures.

Naming is especially complex for a variety of reasons. Often people have an emotional attachment to names or what names represent. When two companies merge, for instance, each wants to retain its company name so it does not appear that either has been taken over. That explains why one sees so many double names like Exxon Mobil, what Siegel refers to as "negotiated names." (If FedEx and UPS were to merge, would they call themselves "FedUp"?) When Citicorp and Travelers merged, they were forced by Citicorp management to use the Citigroup name instead of a completely new name.[132]

It is also difficult to create or find names that can be registered and owned. With the proliferation of new businesses, products and services, intellectual property lawyers play a critical role in protecting clients from lawsuits should they adopt a previously registered name, and in advising on the uncertainties of potential conflicts. Many companies have been embarrassed by overlooking potential conflicts.

Hidden Meanings

Namers must be alert to hidden meanings to ensure that a new name that is supported by the client's marketing department and management isn't freighted with negative associations or meanings, however subtle, especially in different cultures and languages. A notorious example is Chevrolet *Nova*, which to speakers of

Spanish sounds like *no va* or "doesn't go." Locally popular product names, like cheap wines, often don't travel well. Some examples: *Erektus*, a Swedish energy drink; *Super Piss*, the Finnish lock de-icer; Poland's chocolate *Fart* bar and, of course, *Spotted Dick*, an English sponge pudding mix shot through with currants.[133] Don't look for them at your local Wal-Mart. On a recent visit with Siegel & Gale's naming group, a visitor heard a discussion about the merits of a particular name which, while perfectly useful in English, could mean "passing gas" in Korean. The name had even more dire implications in Japanese. These days, brand consultants build market research into the name development process, so that new names meet all strategic and communication objectives, and hidden negatives can be detected.

Further complicating name development are the faulty processes used at most companies to manage the project, and the discomfort and uncertainty many executives exhibit in evaluating naming alternatives. Most people have a visceral reaction to names, and tend to discard them out of hand, especially when colleagues (spouses and companions, too) don't immediately like them. This kind of rampant subjectivity, as opposed to a more disciplined approach to name evaluation, adds significant time and expense to an already daunting task.

Part Art, Part Science

Siegel & Gale is guided by several brand platforms: the business objectives, brand positioning, brand personality and the market dynamics, most notably the naming used by competitors. The quest is for accuracy, simplicity and functionality. The firm strongly recommends retaining names that represent solid assets, in the face of many clients' tendency to seek new names as a solution to looming problems.

As a proponent of simplicity, Siegel prefers names that are real words (rather than abstract or contrived names), that extend the scope and reach of names already owned by the company, or that have a relationship to the company history. Unfortunately, it has become increasingly difficult to avoid creating made-up names in order to get legal registration.[134]

"The task is to find real words that communicate clearly and make good business sense," says Jeff Lapatine, Group Director, Naming & Brand Architecture. He joined the firm 30 years ago to simplify legal documents, and has worked on more than 500 naming projects for Siegel & Gale. Lapatine, a lawyer and onetime Prentice-Hall editor, has seen the naming process grow more sophisticated in the relentless search for everyday words. By default, neologisms become a real option, but as he points out, made-up names require heavy advertising to seat them in the public consciousness.[135]

Name development is more an art than a science. The naming group—some three to six experienced na-mers—brainstorm together, a strategic platform their magnetic north. They conduct client interviews and cre-ate a positioning for the entity to be named, usually no longer than three paragraphs. Based on the positioning, the client is scrutinized for clusters of familiar attributes, or themes, termed "buckets" at Siegel & Gale. From a total of five to seven buckets, themes that overlap at least three buckets are extracted. The business of creating names commences with these dominant themes, until names are winnowed to three, then to one, final candidate for client consideration.[136]

As the project evolves, the naming team conducts sophisticated trademark searches to determine if the name is cleared for use in the U.S., North America or worldwide. A registered name not in current use may be acquired, or possibly applied to a company or product in a completely different genre or geographical area than the originally registered name. And, as many have observed, trademarks can coexist with URLs or websites, until the URL squatter sells the asset. The due diligence process may involve conducting linguistic checks for root words and running computer programs to generate hundreds of name alternatives that match prefigured criteria. In the final analysis, the most effective and memorable names have been drawn out of the collective imaginations and inspirations of the group.

Where Everybody Knows Your Name

Looking over the lengthy list of names Siegel & Gale has introduced into the marketplace, you have to be impressed by the firm's success in creating and registering an array of names for major corporations and products, using real words or ones based on real words. With par-

ent companies in parentheses, the roster includes: Amex
Blvd. (American Express), Capmark (GMAC Commercial
Mortgage), Auro (GoldToe socks), Cordiant, Veridian,
Novartis, Primedia, Masterpiece (Chubb), MasterCard,
Nortel, Magellan (Nortel), MetroCard (MTA), Olight
(DuPont Displays), NexPress (Kodak and Heidelberg),
and CashStream (Mellon). The firm also developed the
"brand architecture," i.e., the naming interrelationship
between products/services and the parent company, for
companies ranging from Yahoo, Morgan Stanley Dean
Witter and United Health Group to Nortel, Stryker, EDS,
Motorola and Boise.

As companies gobble up other companies and new
businesses and services are hatched, the name game becomes more problematic. A tsunami of new names roils
the marketplace. Employees and customers alike are hard
pressed to access, let alone understand, organizations—
what they do and how the mosaic of their activities fits
together; millions of dollars are expended on protecting
product names and services that are in disuse or have no
market equity. Naming incoherence subverts the critical
points of contact that business depends on—contacts with
potential customers, investors, the media and so on—and
inhibits companies from reinforcing their identity and
positioning, according to Siegel.

The Politics of Naming

In virtually all of Siegel & Gale's identity and branding assignments—and the firm has worked for many

kinds of organizations, from global market leaders to not-for-profits to government agencies—Siegel asserts that "creating intelligent brand architecture systems is a critical building block that must be addressed." The job is challenging. "To do this, we must become immersed in the culture of the organization, spend time with the people who run all the business units to learn what they do and get their perspectives, and access any research on hand about their names and product names," he says.[137]

"We work closely with the corporate legal staff to determine the names that are registered, the programs in place to protect trademarks and the attendant costs. Since the ultimate objective is to build a coherent system that resonates with employees and other core audiences, our findings and recommendations will unsettle many people throughout the organization who resist change or feel their jobs are threatened."[138]

Siegel recalls when his firm was presenting its brand architecture proposal to Larry Bossidy, the hard-driving CEO of AlliedSignal. Bossidy asked why two division names were so similar. An Allied executive responded that it was needed to accommodate a fellow executive so he could continue to run his business unit. "This didn't sit well with Mr. Bossidy, who told us to consolidate the two units into one with a name that clearly described what they did," Siegel says. "Unfortunately, not many CEOs get as involved as Mr. Bossidy, or act as decisively. Generally, there are a lot of time-consuming negotiations to resolve such problems."[139]

Chapter 8: Surviving Green Eyes

The model for business communications has shifted from passive to proactive to interactive, from broadcasting to narrowcasting to micromarketing. Information technology provides speed, flexibility and reach, which opens up unprecedented avenues for communications. Faced with such far-reaching changes, corporations . . . are finding that they have to revamp their communications programs completely or get knocked down in the aftershocks. . . . It seems to me, when you cut through all the hype, that the interactive media primarily offer corporations a new means of talking with people—but they demand that they learn to talk with people in a new way. The corporation has to climb down from the speaker's platform of the old, one-way communications model, mingle with the audience and provide people with something extra for their time and attention. As one expert put it, when you're connected, "you're onstage—so do something—fast!" Not exactly most corporations' cup of tea.

—Alan Siegel[140]

Siegel wrote this in the Winter 1996 issue of Design Management Institute's special publication, *Identity in a Digital World,* just a year before the dot-com bubble began to swell. The period 1997–2001 was a heady time, narcotic in its virulence. The Web was the new killer app. Entrepreneurs, mostly young and very bright, started up a slew of Internet businesses, fueled by suddenly available venture capital money, low interest rates, soaring stock prices and speculative investing. With Internet traffic doubling every 100 days, the U.S. Department of Commerce predicted the Internet business would reach $300 billion by 2002.

Blowing Bubbles

The dot-com companies, constructed on questionable new business models, frequently were run by inexperienced managers bent on building brand awareness and winning market share. They gave their products away for free, hoping to recoup later by charging fees. The new entrepreneurs raised money by floating public stock offerings, making those who got in early enough very rich—at least on paper. Few seemed aware that the technology-inspired boom was no different than its predecessors, going back to the railroad boom in the 1840s. Like the booms of yore and the recent past, speculators overvalued the companies until the bubble popped, plunging share prices and many of the new companies into the toilet.[141]

For a while, from January 2001 through August 2001, Siegel & Gale climbed aboard the digital roller coaster and jettisoned a tested business plan, risking its hard-earned reputation as a superb maker of brands. The firm now aspired to become an Internet company, and all that it entailed. The managing partners were not a collection of overweening graspers, but harbored earnest digital intent. The result: Siegel & Gale suffered seriously, edging to the precipice of dissolution. It is not an unfamiliar story in that superheated period of unbridled ambition and irrational exuberance, but it is worth recounting for its object lessons.

Back Story

First, a little back story. In 1985, the steady trajectory of Siegel & Gale's growth as a privately owned corporate identity firm was altered unexpectedly. Martin Sorrell, the CFO of Saatchi & Saatchi plc, the global advertising firm based in London, approached Siegel & Gale to discuss adding them to Saatchi's portfolio of companies. Driven by the ambitious Saatchi brothers, Maurice and Charles, the agency was poised to offer highly attractive acquisition proposals, promising acquired management earn-outs of up to ten times earnings by leveraging United Kingdom accounting rules.

Siegel was intrigued by the irreverent advertising campaigns the Saatchis created in Europe, in particular their political campaign for Margaret Thatcher, and felt that an alliance with them could jump-start his firm's global expansion. He theorized that collaborating with a gaggle of world-class firms could build long-term relationships and secure funding to strengthen the Simplification business.

After a six month-courtship, Siegel agreed to sell the firm to the Saatchi marketing communications empire, which at its zenith had 150 offices in 92 countries, with over 5,000 employees. "Many people in the marketing and advertising community were surprised that a publicly held company purchased a corporate identity firm," Siegel said. While it was exciting at first to be part of a high-profile company in supercharged London, Siegel soon found the Saatchis were in over their heads. Management talent was thin; organizational skills and focus were wanting.

"It turned out to be a pure financial play," according to Siegel. "Over the period they owned us, the Saatchi organization went from one financial crisis to another, eventually splitting up in 1996 into two companies." The following year Siegel negotiated a management buyout with a third party, which provided equity to finance the transaction.[142]

Plausible Reasons

Well before the Saatchi alliance ended, Siegel entertained the idea of going into the digital business in a big way, for plausible reasons. Siegel & Gale has long been a front-runner in adapting new technologies for design and corporate communications. The firm pioneered in the use of high-speed laser printers to make customized statements and forms. For The Chubb Group of Insurance Companies, it designed, in 1984, the first electronically custom-printed insurance package, which led to Siegel & Gale's Simplification experts reengineering documents through publishing interactivity.

"In 1979 when we were creating simplified instructions

and forms for the IRS, our designers produced layouts by hand in pencil," Siegel recalls. "Here were these talented designers with graduate degrees from the Yale School of Design staying all night to produce design concepts by hand." Meanwhile, Siegel & Gale's project teams were compiling corporate identity manuals, massive three-ring binders with up to a dozen sections spelling out in graphic detail the requirements for producing everything from stationery and brochures to signs and identification on trucks.

As digital media presented the realistic opportunity to swap handwork for computers, Siegel & Gale encouraged its employees to experiment with the new software and hardware to improve the firm's capabilities. Says Siegel: "We gave employees state-of-art computers to use in their free time, and they came up with some powerful programs that dramatically improved our new business presentations and allowed us to replace cumbersome identity manuals with dynamic electronic design systems."[143]

To help corporate communications and design managers efficiently use the formats and graphic standards it created for them, Siegel & Gale assembled an interdisciplinary team of programmers, designers and simplifiers, led by Scott Lerman and Tim Leonard, to develop the Electronic Design Director™. The custom software application literally "directs" the making of new designs, automatically selecting appropriate formats and interactively responding to questions about design guidelines. It is a very flexible, responsive training resource, providing beginners and expert designers information at their own levels. EDD can be used as an electronic manual, conserving a great deal of paper. It can also be customized into a correspondence manual or brochure manual for marketing and other departments, applying all the institutionally approved logo placements, templates and guidelines, something that is not available in off-the-shelf programs. Further, EDD sends electronic documents to internal or external printers and can transfer the files elsewhere. EDD proved to be a pioneer in time- and expense-saving communications technology.[144]

The Internet explosion, as it is invariably called, and the commercialization of the Web in the mid-1990s enabled Siegel & Gale to broaden the scope and reach of its branding programs. Moreover, it helped leverage the Simplification group's skills to design accessible interfaces and content, and expand the firm's business to service entrepreneurs planning Internet companies. Steve Dolbow, an experienced IBM executive, was hired to lead the practice, who in turn brought passionate young people aboard.

No-Fault Divorce

"Just as we were generating a lot of business for the digital practice," Siegel says, "our parent company, Saatchi & Saatchi, split into two companies—a stripped-down Saatchi & Saatchi and a new company that we named Cordiant." Saatchi concluded that Siegel & Gale was no longer integral to its core business of global advertising. So it sold the consulting company for $33.8 million in cash back to Siegel & Gale's management and Vestar Capital Partners, a New York investment firm specializing in management buyouts. The divestiture, achieved in 1998, ended Saatchi's 13-year ownership of Siegel & Gale, but offered Siegel the prospect of renewed independence or at least a better fit with another company. Said Siegel: "Independence will give us the flexibility and speed to respond aggressively to new market opportunities, domestically and abroad."[145]

On reflection, Siegel has mixed feelings about the Saatchi period. The association did in fact help Siegel & Gale expand its global reach. The firm opened an office in London and networked with design firms affiliated with Saatchi in major markets. Through these collaborations Siegel & Gale was introduced to British Petroleum, US Steel (which Siegel & Gale renamed USX), and Celanese (Siegel & Gale created the merged identity, Hoechst Celanese). Siegel & Gale also acquired Jim Cross Design, a highly respected design firm with offices in Los Angeles and San Francisco.

But Saatchi was never able to facilitate effective cross-marketing among its holdings, build a common culture, provide training or achieve its financial goals. Saatchi's emphasis was on supporting its stock price in order to underwrite an aggressive acquisition program. Meanwhile, Siegel says, his consulting company was growing and "generating attractive profit margins and doing exciting work in digital media and the Internet." To its credit, Saatchi did not inhibit Siegel & Gale's daily activities, Siegel added.[146]

Green Eyes

Leaving Saatchi, "we saw an opportunity to strike gold because Internet service companies were going public with enormous valuations," Siegel says frankly. "The Siegel & Gale management team was turned on by the prospect of making a significant amount of money through an IPO or a sale to one of the public Internet companies." For a short period, Siegel & Gale's leveraged buyout of its firm from Saatchi made it arguably the largest independent corporate identity consultancy. Moreover, the magazine *Internet Computing*, published by the Institute of Electrical and Electronic Engineers, ranked it among the top 20 interactive media consultancies in the world.[147]

Almost overnight, the focus, character and values of Siegel & Gale were transformed. Siegel calls it the "green eyes period." "The strategic management consultant we hired felt we had no alternative to putting all our resources behind growing the Internet business if, as he said, 'We want to create real wealth for the management.'"

Speaking publicly for the first time about this astonishing shift in fortunes, Siegel's candor is disarming: "We went from a company providing high-level corporate and brand identity programs to senior executives at global companies—to a company that jumped through hoops to secure contracts from Internet entrepreneurs bankrolled with seed money to create new companies, products and services that would 'revolutionize' an industry and generate millions in revenue."[148]

Given Siegel & Gale's credentials—a 30-year history of building iconic brand identities, a veteran Simplification group adept at creating friendly content and interfaces, and world-class graphic designers and video producers—the firm's client roster grew rapidly. Siegel & Gale marketed its capabilities aggressively in hot Internet publications and the *Wall Street Journal*; sponsored NPR's "All Things Considered" radio program; and jointly sponsored a symposium, in San Francisco, on branding and the Internet, with the renowned management consultant Tom Peters and IDEO, a company that espouses innovation through design.

At the 1999 IDEO symposium, Peters praised the art of simplification as practiced by Siegel & Gale for "[taking] something as uninformative and confusing as a credit-card bill and [turning] it into an easy-to-read, easy-to-understand, customer-friendly communications that repositions the bank that sends it out as the kind of financial institution that actually delivers service!" The media exposure generated much new business for Siegel & Gale.[149]

(Ironically, it was Tom Peters in his internationally best-selling book, *In Search of Excellence* [1982], who counseled managers, for a full chapter, to "stick to the knitting—stay with the business that you know"—a cautionary note lost on Siegel & Gale and many other Internet aspirants.)

Market Share Is King

All that really mattered in those tumultuous digital days was generating revenues. "Don't worry about financial overexposure by hiring bodies ahead of revenues or overpaying relatively inexperienced people; just expand office space to accommodate anticipated revenues." That was the tonic of the times, Siegel recalls. Hundreds of hours were spent trying to impress investment bankers and potential buyers, instead of paying attention to properly servicing clients and maintaining profit margins.

"I was amazed that these financial wizards from the investment banks, leveraged buyout firms and even the commercial banks were fascinated by revenue growth, and that they discounted profitability, margins, revenue-per-employee and the longevity of client relationships," Siegel says, still flummoxed after all these years. Apparently, the knock against Siegel & Gale was that the firm was not a "pure play" in the digital arena; incredibly, the firm's annual revenue growth of more than 75 percent was considered "not impressive."[150]

Nevertheless, there were small positives. During the Internet boom, Siegel & Gale worked with hundreds of clients, start-ups that ran the gamut from dating services to auctions, real estate services to catalogues. The firm also aided several longtime clients, like American Express and Ernest & Young, extending their brands online. The remaining Siegel & Gale–built websites of that period are but a handful: Jiffy Lube, the College Board, the Graduate Testing Center and The Weather Channel.

Survivors

In the wake of the burst dot-com bubble, Siegel & Gale faced a crisis: revenue dried up and the firm could not downsize fast enough. The leveraged buyout firm, which had pumped more capital into the firm in exchange for a large hunk of management ownership, butted heads with Siegel & Gale's bank, which promptly cut off the branding firm's line of credit. Remarks Siegel: "Through it all I kept the senior management team in place. They stood by the company, and we eventually sold Siegel & Gale to Omnicom, the largest and most profitable marketing services firm in the world."[151]

Hard lessons were extracted from "green eyes," at the expense of wasted capital and diminished hopes, now downscaled to realistic expectations. Siegel concedes he should have pulled the plug on the venture when the investment specialists "got out of control." His caveats are sensible: "Beware of arrogance, greed and pure bullshit; and beware of phony business plans." Fiscal prudence is clearly essential, he says, as he ticks off a litany of cautionary advice: "Don't rack up fixed overhead expenses in anticipation of increasing revenues. Keep your capital structure in line with growth. It's better to be understaffed in service businesses."[152]

Today it's a different time, psychologically light years away from the Internet bubble. Chastened and wiser,

Siegel now pursues the promises of "relationship technology" in a more measured but no less creative way. "We came out of it and are prosperous again, but not without the unswerving loyalty of our senior staff, ferocious attention to cash management and time-honored business practices, and a fortuitous sale to Omnicom, who recognized the company's future potential."[153]

"What are the residual pluses from that period?" ponders David Srere, Co-Managing Director of Siegel & Gale's New York office, which generates the lion's share of the firm's business. "I think the residual plus is returning to what we do. We are a strategic branding firm, not an Internet firm. Surviving that is obviously a good thing." Asked if losing independence is a bad thing, he responds, "Depends on what day you ask."[154]

Chapter 9: Voice into Brand

I first used "Corporate Voice" when I was working with 3M. Eventually, I transformed Corporate Voice into Brand Voice. In the eighties I started saying that our "deliverable" [results of the consultant's work] was a Brand Voice. That was the umbrella deliverable. Underneath that there was the brand promise, the brand identity, the core messages, and so on—all the elements of branding as we know it today. As branding became a buzzword, the corporate identity business morphed into the branding business. We are practically the only firm that still talks about identity all the time.

—Alan Siegel[155]

Proponents of branding are uncomfortable with dictionary definitions of "brand." Shackling the word to its historic roots rankles them. As far back as the sixteenth century, "to brand" meant burning a mark with a hot iron on, among many things, criminals and bulls.[156] As English is a dynamic, protean language, it is unsurprising that "brands" became "trademarks" on wine casks, liquor, timber, metals and practically all goods except textiles (for good, flammable reasons). Over the centuries, brand came to signify a mark of quality or distinctiveness. The advent of mass-produced packaged goods in the nineteenth century introduced "brand name," which was applied to products and product lines, and protected by trademark law. ("Brand new," however, is 500 years old, derived from "brent new" or "as if fresh from the furnace"; Shakespeare preferred "fire-new.")[157]

The successful brand-maker, Scott Bedbury, a former advertising whiz with Nike and senior vice president of marketing at Starbucks, views brand as a "fundamental essence," a sort of neutral (neither good nor bad) Platonic ideal. From his recent book, *A New Brand World*:

> *A brand is the sum of the good, the bad, the ugly, and the off-strategy. It is defined by your best products as well as your worst product. It is defined by award-winning advertising as well as by the god-awful ads that somehow slipped through the cracks, got approved, and, not surprisingly, sank into oblivion. It is defined by the accomplishments of your best employee—as well as by the mishaps of the worst hire that you ever made. It is also defined by your receptionist and the music your customers are subjected to when placed on hold.*[158]

In Bedbury's formulation, brand is as much about corporate behavior and customer interaction as the quality of what is produced. He is struck by the similarities between defining a person and defining a brand—not unlike the model posited by Siegel a decade earlier. Brands, Bedbury elaborates, "are not physical things that can be held in your hand, placed on your feet, or measured accurately on a scale. Such characteristics belong to products . . . Brands are living concepts that we hold in our minds for years. What goes into them is both logical and irrational."[159]

Brand Wars

Siegel challenges the widespread misuse of the term: "To me a brand is associated with a product, and a corporation is more than a product. There is the Xerox machine, a brand. Yet Xerox is an employer; Xerox is a member of a community; it's much more than a brand. The bigger element of Xerox is their identity—who they are, what they stand for, and why I should do business with them. People are looking to companies to see if they're socially responsible, a good place to work, a good investment. In my opinion, to use 'brand' for a company is inappropriate. Identity is a better term."[160]

Heresy from a leading brand developer? Not really, but it is characteristic of the outspoken Siegel, whose nuanced pronouncements can be vexing were one to "understand him too quickly," to paraphrase André Gide's proviso. "If you're selling toothpaste or liquor—commodity types of products—where there are minor points of differences among them, 'brand' is probably right," Siegel says. "You're trying to decommoditize the product. But a product alone cannot be emblematic of all the attributes of a corporation."[161] Conversely, the absence of generic corporate brands—there are no "private label corporations," unless they are ruses like dummy corporations—suggests that all companies have some kind of culture, whether vivid or bland.

Corporate Voice is Siegel & Gale's proprietary phrase, but it has become an integral part of the vocabulary of branding. Brand-speak, on the other hand, metastasized into the kudzu of identity consulting, spreading everywhere and covering everything. (*FastCompany* magazine diagnosed the ailment as "Obsessive Branding Disorder," declaring that "branding is the self-help industry of corporate America.")[162]

Can an organization be branded by simply sewing a logo onto a baseball cap and distributing it widely? Sports celebrities and entertainers are counseled in the techniques of "personal branding" (or "handling") and marketing to generate "buzz." They consciously dress and speak a certain way, appear tactically at events and support causes appropriate to the desired image they hope to project. Is this brand or merely hype?

Observes Siegel: "The market changed from identity to branding, and what the clients were buying was branding, not identity. I think it's confusing, a disaster. Branding is the most misused, misunderstood and abused term. I've started to talk more about identity and voice than about branding. I find that I spend half my time defining the terms, what branding is and what the value of branding is, even when clients come pre-sold with a brand assignment in hand."[163]

Rather than fight the brand-mania engulfing corporate America, Siegel has chosen to communicate his brand practices through a common language that is understood, however imperfectly, by consultant and client. For better or worse, branding has become that language. Patricia

Deneroff, Group Director, Consulting, for Siegel & Gale, has a similar take on the lax usage of branding. She distinguishes between Corporate Voice of the recent past and Brand Voice as it's now practiced. "Voice," she says, is "a glorious term to encapsulate a belief, once you have identified the brand strategy and how to make sure it is embraced in everything a company says and does. You articulate the brand strategy, or brand promise, and the Voice becomes the expression of it. That to me is the definition of a corporate brand."[164]

$E=mc^2$

New York Co-Managing Director Srere is blunt about his understanding of "brand" and "voice." "There isn't any difference between Corporate Voice and Brand Voice," he says, adding: "The distinctions we ourselves make are distinctions only dogs can hear. It's about the voice of an organization." Siegel & Gale's competitive edge, he asserts, is, "We simplify. Others are formulaic. We have no aspiration to become a big, stupid branding firm. Our idea of the business is to build big global master brands. Simplicity is our valued-based philosophy: we help our clients simplify. Simple is smart. We produce work that is clear, fresh, inspiring and useful."

Srere's criteria for taking on new clients are simple enough. "We ask ourselves, can we make money on the project? Will the assignment enhance our portfolio? And are our people going to have fun? It's very rare that you get all three; you look for two or three," he says. Adhering to the elegance of simplicity, Srere uses Einstein's famous equation for mass-energy equivalence as a metaphor for the Siegel & Gale approach to branding. "$E=mc^2$ is unique. Brands that are clear, fresh, honest, inspiring and useful—that's Siegel & Gale's $E=mc^2$."[165]

The Voice Within

For Deneroff, Voice has a "much more robust consequence" than just communication. "It's not only about how you communicate but also about how you behave, and that gets into values implementation. Voice is at play, in every single minute, from how you answer the phone to what a piece of communications looks like. The positioning is the result of a study we do to articulate the essence of a brand, what makes it special. That is a fairly deliberate process to arrive at a brand definition."[166]

Comparing the way Siegel & Gale addresses brand, with, for example, advertising agencies, she says, "Theirs is a much more external-directed exploration; it's more about the trends in the marketplace and what the customer or prospective customer wants. Ours is much more 'foundational,' in the true sense of what constitutes the identity of the corporation or institution. And it starts, so profoundly, with the internal discovery process, because we believe the truth of an organization resides within."

This explains why Siegel & Gale, as a consulting firm with a unique branding process, spends so much time learning about a corporation or institution, because the locus of the brand idea usually is there. "Then," says

Deneroff, "we poke our heads outside and look at the trends in the market, what a particular customer group wants, and at other externals, such as what others in the peer group are doing." The area of opportunity, as she sees it, "is that overlap of the client's unique strengths and outside needs, *which defines the expression of the brand promise*" [emphasis added]. These days many consultants claim to aspire to a "more scientific view," and talk of brand valuation, brand metrics and stock valuation. "For us, I like a simpler definition: what's the unique value of an organization? That's what the brand is. Alan doesn't like the term 'branding' because others have appropriated it and use it in a diminutive and imprecise way."[167]

Siegel likes to say that he didn't spring "brand identity" on anybody; the market sprung it on him.[168] Responding to the market's need for a branding vernacular without compromising its "Simple is smart" patrimony, Siegel & Gale refined Corporate Voice into Brand Voice, reinforcing the concept with a clarity of analysis and expression that pierces twenty-first-century media clutter and rises above the clamor. Insiders believe that at its core, Siegel & Gale is The Simplification Company in all but name.

In truth, Siegel & Gale's new capabilities literature is a little like the movie *Back to the Future*. The firm reduces its tasks to *Simplify*, *Amplify* and *Exemplify*. Simplification is getting down to the essence of an organization and what it stands for. Or, as Deneroff says, "How do we help organizations understand, in the simplest and purest way, how they add value? That is what distinguishes Siegel & Gale: the tradition of Simplification.

Whether Simplification is a separate practice or an ethos, or whether it's a methodology, it is not practiced by other branding firms."[169] Amplification is the communications process: getting the word out. Exemplify, in Srere's words, is "walking the walk; living the brand." "Brand can no longer reside in the marketing department," he declares. "You're not going to get anything done [there]. Aligning behavior and process requires bravery. Employees should be evaluated in terms of what they contribute to the brand. They should be hired and offered incentives to vivify the brand."[170]

Branding Principles and Disciplines

The consulting firm's credo remains strong and steadfast, yet supple and visionary, as evidenced in its responses to requests for branding proposals. Three principles continue to guide Siegel & Gale after 35 years:

*We are committed to using **breakthrough simplicity** to create clear, coherent, compelling brands.*

*The real value of a brand is its ability to **close the gap between promise and delivery.***

*Brand solutions must respond to the **practical business needs** of our clients.*

"Breakthrough simplicity" means getting at the heart, the *distinctive truth*, of an organization. Fact, not fiction

or wishful thinking, guides the analysis and recommendations. There is a narrative to virtually every brand, a
story to uncover and relate in believable tropes and plain
English. (Asked about the future of metrics in measuring brand efficiency, Srere says, "We're in the business
of storytelling. We're the marriage of art and science.
When branding is done properly, it's one of the factors
that drives stock price.")[171]

In its brief to clients, Siegel & Gale wants to create
"brands that understand and communicate what customers want with pinpoint accuracy, and deliver solutions
with unerring consistency." These are high standards
and, of course, Siegel & Gale itself cannot achieve them.
It raises the bar to help *clients* transcend their aspirations
to make an important difference to their customers, employees and owners.

The "gap between promise and delivery" recalls T.S.
Eliot's memorable lines in the poem "The Hollow Men":
*Between the idea / And the reality / Between the motion /
And the act / Falls the Shadow.*[172] Eliot portrayed the
gap between imagination and reality as one very hard
to negotiate. The "shadow"—whether it's inertia or lack
of clarity—must be overcome. Narrowing that distance
leads to creating successful brands.

"Responding to practical business needs" indicates that
the firm's recommendations will be real and executable;
they will help clients reach their objectives; and they are
cost-effective. This is right out of Business 101.

The services offered by Siegel & Gale by and large are
simple, transparent, logically grouped and clear. (When

Irene Etzkorn, the firm's most experienced language simplifier, was asked recently for Siegel & Gale's "glossary of branding terms," she replied they didn't have one; the terminology, she says, "better be clear to everyone.")

Siegel & Gale's current services, as pulled from the firm's website, include:[173]

Brand Identity Services, i.e., Brand Strategy, Naming, and Visual Identity Systems, the last being a more accurate description of the graphic elements of what was called Corporate Identity.

Communications Services broadly range from writing and other editorial services to creating booklets and other "leave behind" material, graphic design, advertising and packaging, new product and service introductions, and corporate films.

Brand Alignment closes the gap between the promise and performance with employee education programs and attitude studies.

Simplification involves plain language writing projects, information and document design, simplification blueprints (instructional material), and distribution strategies.

Brand Research gathers hard data for name development, brand equity (the total valuation of the brand, i.e., customer loyalty and satisfaction, the quality of products and services, both financial and non-financial assets), audience segmentation, and researching consumers and business-to-business interaction through focus groups. The firm also evaluates visual identity systems and does benchmarking and tracking studies.

Interactive Media—which the company introduced

into its practice years before the Internet explosion—creates websites, intranets/extranets, interactive kiosks, various training tools and wireless applications.

Breakthrough Brands

Siegel & Gale's process of locating and expressing the unique qualities of client brands evolved organically. Brand Strategy is developed methodically through four actions: *Discover, Define, Dramatize,* and *Measure* the strategy.

First, Siegel & Gale audits client communications relative to its competition, conducts interviews, benchmarking studies and brand equity research to *discover* as much as it can about current strategies, and then summarizes the findings to management. Next, using research, it *defines* the client's positioning and creates a testable "messaging matrix." Depending on client needs, the consulting firm *dramatizes* its proposed solutions, developing a visual system or various marketing directions, and tests these for validity. Finally, it *measures* the effectiveness of the preferred brand strategy through research.

An outgrowth of Corporate Voice, the present branding process is invested with more diagnostic and validating research, and stresses measurable results and aftercare for intelligent course correction. Siegel says that Brand Strategy is more attuned than ever to the "touchpoints" between the brand and customers and key constituencies.

"Breakthrough brands," as Siegel calls them, pierce the

cacophony of competing brand claims and promises by precisely articulating and memorably communicating their own brand's essence, and living up to customer expectations, as these selected case histories demonstrate:[174]

Boise. Under its former name, Boise Cascade, the company was best known for manufacturing paper, despite diversification into building materials and office products. Siegel & Gale was hired to develop a brand strategy, naming and brand architecture solution that could correct public misperceptions. The result: Boise became the official corporate name, and the company adopted a new bold identity. The tree symbol was dropped because it represented a focus limited to paper making. Boise adopted a messaging platform around its new tagline, *Work. Build. Create.* Applying the brand strategy, Siegel & Gale redesigned Boise's website to showcase key principles shared across all of its businesses.[175]

SunTrust, one of the largest commercial banks in the U.S., cherished its "geographic footprint" in the Southeast as its greatest asset. But increased competition, product commoditization, confused customers and disparate employee subcultures from acquired local bank charters clouded its brand visibility. Siegel & Gale helped identify SunTrust's core values and distinctive culture that drove past successes through exhaustive employee and client research. Customers loved the bank and its local flavor but were unaware of SunTrust products and services they weren't using. To leverage the spirit of customer advocacy as an institutional promise, Siegel & Gale developed the brand positioning *Not just at your service—at your side*, created new Common Mission and Values Statements, a restructured brand architecture, and a new corporate identity. The new brand strategy debuted in 1,500 retail branches, backed with retail signage, interactive solutions, communications and process simplification and a cross-selling incentive program. Said SunTrust's chief marketing officer: "Siegel & Gale helped us understand what it is about our people that makes us who we are. And then they showed us how to translate that spirit into how we talk and behave as an organization."

The New School, an atypical university in New York City's Greenwich Village, was founded in 1919 as The New School for Social Research to promote global peace and justice. Its eight unique schools include a leading liberal arts and social policy school, a vocational design school, and schools for music, drama and jazz. After perceptual studies of the university, including an online, interactive open-ended query of students that drew an astonishing 40 percent response rate, Siegel & Gale advised changing the university's name, in 2004, to the more communicative "The New School." Originally brought in to help the university communicate its mission, Siegel & Gale crafted a new positioning and a new brand architecture, linking The New School with the names of its component colleges. A nontraditional palette of warm-spectrum colors and bold advertising revitalized the university's identity. Citing its schools' shared values and goals, New School President Bob Kerrey said, "Linking the name of each school with the name of the university, without losing the individual identity, reflects this important dynamic."[176] The new positioning: "The New School was founded on the proposition that a free society depends on free expression. That learning has its roots in creativity as well as discipline and critical intelligence. That training people in the skills they need to make democracy succeed means giving them the courage to express their own distinctive voices."

Chapter 10:

Fulfilling Brand Expectations

The big change in branding today is that people finally realize that if you position a company and have a brand promise, then you have to deliver on it. The experience has to match the expectations. You have to train the organization to behave in a manner that reinforces and aligns with the brand promise. That's the biggest change in the last five, eight years. People like Steve Jobs, who runs Apple Computers, have vision. They inculcate that vision in the company. People come to work there because they believe in the vision, and they behave in a manner that reinforces that vision. Howard Schultz, the chairman of Starbucks, has great vision, and he executes it magnificently. Any time you deal with Starbucks, there is a consistency of brand experience. The people who work there are trained to deliver on the Starbuck's brand promise. For the vast majority of companies, that's not true. They make representations in advertising and communications that they don't deliver on.

—Alan Siegel[177]

Can any company find or create its brand? Siegel believes so. "I've worked with literally a thousand companies, and I found very few situations where I couldn't identify a thread to build a true expression of what the company stands for and how it's different," he says. "Most companies have a history, and the people who run them have a point of view; they have somewhat of a vision." But he quickly adds that as some industrial companies undergo serial mergers, "there's nothing [no vision] there, so you have to make the brand aspirational, and you build it on the vision of the new leader."[178]

An aspirational brand can become real with enough perspiration behind it—i.e., motivation by workable ideas, a strong will at the top and engaged employees everywhere; and, oh yes, a budget commensurate with the effort. "Much depends on the kind of culture the company wants to promote or the way they want to differentiate themselves from a major competitor and stand out in the marketplace," Siegel says. "The critical thing," he warns, "is if the brand promise isn't true or they can't deliver on it. If the company is not willing to spend on training employees to understand how the positioning is reflected in their behavior toward their publics, then it's just window dressing." Siegel believes "the vast majority of branding programs are window dressing because companies don't have the discipline."[179]

Brand promises fail, first of all, because companies "don't do a good job of developing a positioning statement that is well thought out and definitive." Siegel summarizes the lengths to which his firm goes to realize a workable positioning: "When we do a positioning for a company or institution, we learn in our audit what its key communications and messages are. Then we show them how if they adopted our positioning, they could revise their messages . . . their letter to shareholders; the theme of their annual report; how the CEO might refocus his speech he gave last year at the Detroit Economic Club." Concrete suggestions based on the new positioning are applied to employee newsletters, customer call centers, to all the communications that articulate the Brand Voice. The client is presented with a comprehensive blueprint of workable ideas that can then be tested for validity. To ensure that the concepts are widely understood by internal groups in order to win their buy-in, the idea of "brand voice" and the "brand platform" often is summarized in a Brand Voice Book that is distributed to employees.[180]

Six Strategic Insights

Illustrating Siegel's point about the crucial nature of brand promises is a sampling of several his firm developed.[181]

Girl Scouts: **Where girls grow strong**

"Where girls grow strong" is a return to the roots of the Girl Scouts organization. It is the simple, basic strategic insights that cut through the familiar rituals—the uniforms, the badges and, yes, the cookies—to the underlying and entirely contemporary purpose of this ever-relevant movement.

Lehman Brothers: Where vision gets built

Lehman's strategy was to change the dialogue, to go from the expected listing of familiar banking services to the fundamental mission of investment banking—from what the bank could do for its clients to what the clients got out of the bank. "Where vision gets built" is not about financial manipulations, it's about helping visionaries raise the capital to change the world.

Berklee college of music: Nothing conservatory about it

Berklee isn't Julliard. It is a freer, wider-ranging, more thoroughly professional institution that doesn't share the narrow European limits of traditional conservatories. "Nothing conservatory about it" is a declaration of independence, a strategic reassertion of what makes Berklee different, authentic and appealing to the broadest range of students.

3M: Innovation

"Innovation" is a simple, bold reminder of the core idea that drives 3M. It is the common denominator that unites the company's tens of thousands of employees and its equally numerous products. It is a strategic differentiator that grows, like all successful strategies, from the truth of what the company delivers.

CNBC: **Make it your business**

"Make it your business" links the two essential components of the CNBC experience. It ties news to business. And it shows why CNBC's fearless and objective emphasis on sound reporting is a critical necessity for making sound, successful business choices.

Dow: **Living, improved daily**

Dow's strategic insight was to shift the focus from the process to the benefit. Instead of listing all the chemicals that it produced, Dow went directly to what these essentials do for daily life. Instead of lingering on substances, Dow spoke of making fundamental changes in the way that people live.

Another reason brand promises fail is they frequently are not "aligned" to or reinforced by employee behavior. Employees must understand and support the brand, feel they are essential to its success, and be engaged in the process. This requires employee training and effective internal communications to ensure that the right message is disseminated. Alignment can't be achieved with perfunctory management or with outside experts alone; CEOs must be involved, stoking the passion for superior performance in customer relations. They can never relax their hands on the brand engine throttle.

"The marketing and communications programs that companies mount to support their brands essentially offer a promise to the customer," Siegel argues, and gives examples: Target—"Expect more/pay less"; GE—"Imagination at work"; and Wal-Mart—"Always low prices. Always." "We say that the brand definition provides the direction for thinking, communicating and behaving," Siegel emphasizes. High-visibility brands, the ones atop the brand rating charts compiled by business magazines and trade groups, usually are backed with hefty ad budgets and public relations support to build awareness for the brand and what it promises. Whatever the company's size and ad budget, the key for Siegel is that the "brand delivers on the promise, what is often referred to as brand alignment." Mincing no words, Siegel says most brands are "not distinguished, poorly regarded and not visible." His final word: "A brand won't stand for anything positive unless it stands for something meaningful, is promoted and delivers a positive experience. If a brand doesn't define itself, the marketplace will do it on its own."[182]

Chapter 11: After Words

Branding as a Profession

This book is a snapshot taken on the run of Alan Siegel: how he does branding, and what branding offers as a career—a Working Biography. Taking a reductive approach to describing a relatively new, polymathic discipline like branding doesn't do the subject justice. Siegel, wisely perhaps, is reluctant to predict where the business may be headed. But he does offer candid advice to both young people and the more experienced who passionately want to enter this creative, dynamic, challenging field.

Education

Like other large branding consultancies, Siegel & Gale regularly interviews college graduates, increasingly those with MBAs. Most recent college graduates aspiring to enter branding have liberal arts degrees, business degrees or degrees in communications. Many of them interned with or had summer jobs in the business world. Typically, MBAs work from two or five years before starting graduate school.[183]

Firms that provide branding services—advertising agencies, public relations companies and direct response groups—hire people with specialized degrees in graphic design, Internet design, video and film production. For its

Simplification business, Siegel & Gale actively recruits at Carnegie Mellon, RPI and a number of MBA programs to find people who are trained in process simplification, information design, technical writing, cognitive psychology and computer science.[184]

For mid-level and senior staff positions in brand strategy and project management, Siegel & Gale recruits people who have worked in account management at advertising agencies, management consulting firms, and brand marketing and brand management in corporations. Siegel also seeks people with experience in technology, health care, consumer markets, industrial marketing, financial services and not-for-profit organizations.

PhDs in branding and marketing tend to become academics. They also may operate brand centers, conduct research programs and consult privately. They publish business books, some quite successful, and expound their ideas on the lecture circuit and in media appearances. Branding firms, including Siegel & Gale, as well as their clients, use them for special assignments, such as measuring branding impact through ROI (return on investment), an important and growing trend in branding.[185]

Skills for Brand Strategists

To work as a brand strategist for a consulting firm is a challenging assignment requiring a number of sophisticated skills, including these abilities specified by Siegel:[186]

- Analyze and synthesize a mountain of information
- Generate meaningful insights and critical data from management interviews and market research with key audiences
- Write clear and convincing reports and presentations
- Create brand strategies that define and differentiate the product/service or corporation
- Collaborate with demanding clients, firms that work for clients, and creative people
- Maintain the integrity of the strategy in the face of risk-averse client committees or work groups

"Designers, writers and producers have to learn to translate brand strategies into powerful and relevant communications," Siegel says. "They are part of a problem-solving team who can add value by developing concepts that are original, clear and memorable. The successful designers I have worked with are articulate, strong presenters and flexible."

He characterizes successful simplifiers as people who tend to be studious, patient, logical and creative. They are challengers and problem solvers, experimenters and synthesizers, and above all, they write clearly.[187]

Hiring Filters

Every company maintains its particular hiring filters—the general standards and employer preferences that job candidates must negotiate to win a position. Siegel's include Education, Job Experience, Passion,

Communications Skills, Presence, Creativity, References and the Job Interview. Elaborating on the last item, Siegel says, "I look for people who have done their homework before they come to see us . . . what they know about our firm, the branding business, the work we have done, our competitors, what work attracts them, and other insights they might have researched. They should have studied our website, checked out *BrandWeek, Ad Age* and other trade publications, and scanned some books on branding."[188]

Interestingly, Siegel has hired senior people who were *not* college graduates, but they are the rare exception. He considers sales the best training ground for marketing and branding, especially people in already productive careers. "They are in the trenches and learn what motivates the trade and customers," he observes. "Some of them haven't attended college, but I wouldn't hesitate to hire them." He also responds to people with certain unique skills, points of view or experience. For example, he once hired the development director of a renowned modern dance company who became adept at new business development. Ever the basketball fan, Siegel says: "If Dr. J inquired about working for Siegel & Gale in a management or business development position, I would hire him in a New York minute."[189] (This may, or may not, be a joke.)

Siegel tries to hire two types of people: those with a passion for branding and the ability to orchestrate large, complex, global projects, and individuals with specialized skills; for example, in market research and document and graphic design. Brand strategists constitute the core of the company. Everything the firm does grows out of the strategies they create and the client relationships they build. Effective strategists develop distinctive brand programs, manage contracts with clients and bring in new business. Their experience is evident in their command of client presentations, the ability to deal with difficult situations, even in their sense of humor.

The specialists ply their own expertise and partner with outside specialized firms, which provide a range of services, from research and event marketing to financial relations. A major part of the job of the staff specialist is to evaluate and interpret outside work for Siegel & Gale's project teams, ensuring that objectives are met and conflicts or confusion between vendor and buyer are resolved.

The majority of Siegel & Gale's assignments during the last ten years have been global. Project teams travel extensively to conduct on-site interviews and immerse themselves in foreign businesses and cultures. Siegel places a premium on job candidates with a global perspective, people who have studied and traveled abroad, and are multi-lingual. To enrich staff knowledge of global businesses and foreign cultures, he tries to rotate employees from his international offices to the U.S., and vice-versa. English is clearly the language of international business, but not in the marketplace. "Business meetings generally are conducted in English," Siegel explains, "but the strategies and communications must be translated into the culture and language of each country."

In the end, most people enter a business or profession for the personal satisfaction it provides them, not the pay package. It is instructive to read the satisfactions Siegel derives from branding:

Problem solving
Intellectual challenge
Dialogue with smart people
Innovation
Learning
Mentoring
Making a difference
Building the Siegel & Gale brand

Few of the above job benefits appear in the agate type of help wanted ads or headhunters' job descriptions.

A Siegel Quotation Sampler

Seldom in the last 30 years have articles on a major branding developments appeared in large-circulation newspapers or trade publications without an Alan Siegel quote. His phone number is engraved in reporters' Rolodexes® everywhere. His surefire wit and wisdom are sought assiduously by those writing on deadline, though not always appreciated by a company owning or controlling his firm, because his candor occasionally ticks off sister companies and clients. Herewith, a sampling of Siegelisms:

City Condom. New York City announced plans, early in 2006, to release an official city condom "with unique packaging." Bearing in mind that a company already markets a condom with an Empire State Building design, Siegel, when asked what the condom might be called, replied, "City Planner." —*The New York Times*, Feb.15, 2006

Glamour-Challenged New Jersey. At a cost of $260,000 to an image consultant, the state of New Jersey rejected several proposed negative state slogans, including "New Jersey: We'll Win You Over" and "New Jersey: Not as Bad as You Think." Siegel thought the slogans were pretty bad, remarking, "Other than 'I Love New York,' which was magic, I don't think any of these city or state or national slogans make any difference. Usually, it's a way to chuck away money." —*The New York Times*, Nov. 2, 2005

Hell's Bells. After the SBC-AT&T merger, SBC declared it would assume the AT&T name, one of the world's most recognized brands. More concerned with customer service, Siegel said that, in the end, "It's not what they say—it's what they do" that matters. —*The New York Times*, Oct. 28, 2005

Fat Chance. The first lawsuit blaming fast-food companies for not disclosing the health risks of their high-calorie foods was laughed at, but not by Siegel. Paraphrased in the *Times*, he suggested new advertising wasn't the answer; repositioning their brands to represent healthier choices, smaller servings and more health information could actually "strengthen their businesses." —*The New York Times*, Dec. 2, 2002

Craft's Last Gasp. The American Craft Museum asked Siegel, then one of its board members, to rebrand the institution, because similar museums and museum departments were lopping off the word "craft" from their names. Siegel said the job could be done in ten minutes. A half a year of no results later, Siegel conducted some focus groups and concluded that "the negative associations for craft were so great that no amount of money could effectively overcome them." His favorite survey comment was, "Craft can never shed its macramé potholder image, no matter what's done." —*The New York Times*, March 30, 2005

I'm Going to Comcastland. Asked to comment on a proposed name, Comcast Disneyland, were Comcast to take over the Walt Disney Company, Siegel said that many companies emerging from such takeovers are negatively named. His examples were AOL Time Warner; Exxon Mobil, Morgan Stanley, Dean Witter, Discover & Company, Pricewaterhouse Coopers, and "the one I think is the worst," Kyocera Mita. — *The New York Times*, Feb. 13, 2004

There Goes My Heart. With much fanfare as she began her Caesars Palace run in Las Vegas, chanteuse Celine Dion, who helped sell the movie *Titanic* with her lilting song, "My Heart Will Go On," was tapped to become spokesperson for Chrysler. Siegel thought that Chrysler might not be the right vehicle. "They think she's classy?" he was quoted. "I think she's popular and very recognizable and has a certain presence." He did concede she would be largely immune to the problems of such celebrity endorsers as Martha Stewart . . . or O.J. Simpson. — *The New York Times*, Nov. 5, 2002

Don't Doubt Thomas. The death of Wendy's International founder, R. David Thomas, gave the fast food chain's brand keepers much to chew on. (After Col. Harland Sanders died, Kentucky Fried Chicken replaced the Colonel's iconic name and face with KFC, and failed to revive his image with actors, ultimately settling for a caricature of the Colonel.) Siegel thought the original Thomas imagery portrayed "the unique qualities of the Wendy's brand through a person who was folksy, real, human, honest." He counseled Wendy's, at least in the press, "to try to perpetuate the legacy, the values, that Dave Thomas stood for," and cautioned: "I'd definitely stay away from making Dave into a cartoon." —*The New York Times*, Jan. 9, 2002

Hang On, Snoopy, Hang On. The death of Peanuts® creator, Charles M. Schulz, seemed to jeopardize the use of Snoopy and his kooky circle of friends in Metropolitan Life Insurance Company's ads, blimps and promotions, which began in 1985. Siegel called Peanuts "an icon, but a static icon in the future. I can't see it as a viable advertising expression, because advertising has to be topical and responsive to what's happening in the marketplace. . . . I would figure a way to transition out of it." The short of it is that MetLife retained Snoopy as it mascot—even on the blimp—and may reach 100 million customers by 2010. —*The New York Times*, Feb. 17, 2000

Call for Al-Tri-Ah. Despite significant business diversification into packaged food and brewing, Philip Morris Companies kept its nicotine-stained name until 2002 when it switched to a freshly coined name, Altria (Latin "altus" meaning "high," though not necessarily in a mood-altering way). "Strategically, it's a very smart move to change the name," said Siegel at the time of the announcement. "The invisible word behind Philip Morris is 'tobacco,' and they want to project a bigger, broader identity." —*The New York Times*, Nov. 18, 2001

To Heir Is Human. Anxious to join Lee Iacocca in the pantheon of car spokespersons, William Clay Ford, Jr., Ford's CEO, literally became the face of the Ford Motor Company in 2002. Not that there's a cause-and-effect connection, but two years later Ford has been surpassed by Toyota as the second biggest carmaker, which leads to Siegel's quote at the time: "It's nice that there's a heritage, but the heritage has backfired. What are you going to do to bring value to the company? That's what I want to know." —*The New York Times*, Feb. 20, 2002

It's Time to Move Forward. Back in 1990, Toyota Motor Corporate Services of North America decided to fend off anti-Japanese advertising by running an ad campaign about what Toyota does in America, besides manufacturing good vehicles. Opined Siegel: "People want to know what companies are doing and how it will work to the public's advantage. If a campaign like Toyota's is done well, it will create the public impression of a caring company." —*The New York Times*, Oct. 2, 1990. (Toyota constructed a self-image as a compassionate company, telling emotional stories about sponsoring scholarships through the United Negro College Fund. On the Fortune Global 500, published July 24, 2006, Toyota is ranked as the eighth biggest company, one place ahead of Ford.)

Witnesses

Two phrases came to be identified with Alan and his firm that differentiate him and his brand consultancy. One is "Simple is smart"—a perfect expression of Alan's instinctive need for clarity, disdain for jargon, restless desire for straightforward answers, and promise to clients not to waste their time with tortured logic and ornate recommendations. His goal was always to be able to draw a line—straight and true—from description of context to characterization of issues to statement of premises to articulation of conclusions to presentation of implications to creation of expressions. A comprehensive brand strategy had to be as clear and logical as a simple bar chart. That was smart. The theme also knitted the brand strategy and design with the simplified communications practice that distinguishes Siegel & Gale to this day. The second phrase is, of course, "Brand Voice," the organizing model for Siegel & Gale's client engagements and the promised deliverable of the firm's work . . . It is his hallmark concept. Long before others were speaking of a company's brand as products and services, as well as marketing and communications, Alan spoke of brand as the sum total of all expressions and experiences—the brand's voice in the marketplace. He argued that the more unique and compelling that voice, the stronger and more valuable the brand.

*It is a simple, powerful idea, perfectly matched to
Alan's craving for simple, powerful solutions.*
—*Claude Singer, a partner of Lippincott Mercer
and former Siegel & Gale executive*[190]

Alan Siegel's place in marketing history is secure,
judging by this generous assessment of his life's work,
and others like it. Charles Reisler, another former colleague, concurs: "There's no father of anything, but
Alan's had those two breakouts, Voice and Language
Simplification."[191]

The estimable Herb Schmertz, who ran Mobil Oil's
corporate communications for 20 years, lauds Siegel as
a brand-builder who makes "bold recommendations."
"Alan is extremely self-assured and rarely exhibits any self-
doubt. He is able to take complex things and make them
understandable. He sees things that others don't, and is
able to translate his vision into programs."[192]

Eva Hardy, senior vice president of Dominion
Resources, one of the largest integrated energy companies in the U.S., found working with Siegel to effect their
brand change to be a "positive, very painless, constructive
process, with clearly defined suggested actions." Entering
the precincts of an old Virginia company dating to George
Washington's era, the "New York consultant" quickly put
management at ease and "did an extraordinary job in
eliciting from us what our real brand is."[193]

Not all competitors, clients or staff gush so about
Siegel. He is notorious for his low threshold for boredom.
"He does not want to sit through lengthy discussions," a

current employee says. "He doesn't suffer fools gladly and wants very much to get to the heart of the matter." "Drift off into unwarranted digression or messy jargon and he'll call you on it," says another person who worked closely with him. Indeed, a colleague jokes that Siegel is "the only man who turned a case of attention deficit disorder into a brilliantly successful career."

However, a current senior staff member notes that people can underestimate Siegel because he is in their face with piercing questions. "He is a contrarian, challenging preconceived ideas," the executive says. "If you can't keep up with him, he is not very interested in slowing down. Like a butterfly, he moves from idea to idea, and has turned that into his advantage." Says another Siegel & Gale executive: "I think that Alan believes with Emerson that 'nothing great was ever achieved without enthusiasm.' The importance of what Alan does is the passion he has for the craft; he believes in his impact and value."

There is the matter of Siegel's perceived vanity, his "dashing presence," and his custom-made suits accessorized with silver-tipped western belts—at least back when business people actually wore suits and ties to work. An ex-Siegel & Gale senior employee who bought his own clothing from thrift stores was bemused to hear Siegel "natter on" with his modishly attired partner, Bob Gale, about the latest styles in *Esquire*. Without a trace of irony, another former employee thinks of Siegel as the "Donald Trump of Branding," alluding, however, to his media skills, not The Donald's lubricated hairstyle. There is little doubt about it: Siegel, he has style—but, he would hasten to add, not a personal brand.

Siegel certainly has presence. Friends say he exudes confidence and authority, laced with a dollop of modulated chutzpah. "He's a pure human being, an icon for fair play," a source said, recalling an incident witnessed on a subway ride with him. As seems only to happen in New York, a strutting, ranting "bruiser" menaced the passengers, until Siegel "stood up to the wise guy and liquidated the guy's aggressiveness with nothing but his persona."

Again, the sports thing: "Alan was the prototypical jock—I wouldn't call him a 'dumb jock'—but he was a jock, and then developed his intellect," says a friend, attorney Henry Petchesky. He has known Siegel since they were teenagers when Siegel called and caught his pitches on the baseball field. Somewhat aware of Siegel's professional accomplishments, Petchesky most admires Siegel's enterprise. "In those days people didn't take chances, but Alan did. He had a vision about starting his own company, and he did it in his twenties. That takes a lot of balls. His was a natural talent; he was a leader, on the ball field and in life."[194]

Siegel's wife, Gloria, the one person who undoubtedly knows him best, believes he will never quite retire. Describing her husband as an "effective leader, but not a follower," Gloria suggests that politics and academia, two of his interests, would "drive him crazy" because he disdains "decisions by consensus." "He may pass over the reins, but never the involvement. I can see him writing, or consulting privately, but his heart will always be with the company." Siegel will be remembered, she says, "as a straight shooter and original thinker . . . a compassionate human being who genuinely cares about the people he works with and for."[195]

Anecdotes do not make for a rounded portrait, especially in a tightly allocated space. We can only hope that informed observations help triangulate some facets of Siegel's personality. As shown in the text, photography remains Siegel's window on the world. "I am consumed by constructing visual images of things I see in my daily life and travels, and by ideas for communicating messages," he says. "Over the years I have served on the photography boards of major museums, spent time with leading curators and attended hundreds of gallery openings."

Photography books are piled high in his apartment den, and clutter his Madison Avenue office. Two of them he produced: *One Man's Eye: Photographs from the Alan Siegel Collection*, published by Harry N. Abrams, in 2000, and *Step Right This Way: The Photographs of Edward J. Kelty*, with a text by Miles Barth, Alan M. Siegel and Edward Hoagland, published by Barnes & Noble in 2002. Of the latter, the American Library Association's *Booklist* wrote: "The successor to Barth and Alan's eye-popping *One Man's Eye* (2000) is also concerned with a particular person's vision, this time not photo collector Siegel's but that of a professional banquet photographer with a sideline in circus publicity. . . . [Kelty's circus pictures] are scrumptious, sometimes outrageous eye-candy."[196]

Siegel warmly refers to his valuable photos, which he started collecting in the 1960s, as "old friends." He brings them from his apartment to his office, where they are exhibited in rotating fashion, and deposits other images in his daughter Stacy's home in Los Angeles. A few years ago he started making digital photos, and now is attempting to master Adobe Photoshop. Besides photography and branding, and two grandchildren who occupy a special place in his wife Gloria's and his busy life, Siegel serves on several boards reflecting his lifelong interests: the Author's Guild, Museum of Arts and Design, Aperture Foundation (fine art photography), and The American Theatre Wing. ATW, which sponsors the Tony Awards®, affords Siegel, a Tony voter, the privilege of experiencing many Broadway shows. He continues doing pro bono branding and communications work for modern dance companies, environmental groups and health care foundations. At age 68, his thick black hair flecked with silver, Siegel, though carrying the added weight of age, looks as fit as a man fifteen years younger. That he still competes in national rowing contests, plays tennis and kayaks—despite the aches of an active life—backs up his assertion that "sports are a very integral part of my life." 'Twas ever thus.[197]

Selected Reading

Branding

Bedbury, Scott, with Stephen Fenichell. *A New Brand World: 8 Principles for Achieving Brand Leadership in the 21st Century.* NY: Viking Penguin, 2002.

Carter, David E. *American Corporate Identity 2006.* NY: Collins Design, 2005.

Chajet, Clive. *Image by Design: From Corporate Vision to Business Reality.* NY: McGraw-Hill, 1997.

Gregory, James R. *Branding Across Borders: A Guide to Global Brand Marketing.* NY: McGraw-Hill, 2001.

Kelly, Francis, and Barry Silverstein. *The Breakaway Brand: How Great Brands Stand Out.* NY: McGraw-Hill, 2005.

Marconi, Joe. *The Brand Marketing Book: Creating, Managing and Extending the Value of Your Brand.* Lincolnville, IL: NTC Business Books, 2000.

Morris, Evan. *From Altoids to Zima: The Surprising Stories Behind 125 Famous Brand Names.* NY: Simon & Schuster, 2004.

Olins, Wally. *Wally Olins. On Br®nd.* London: Thames & Hudson, 2004.

Schultz, Don E., and Beth E. Barnes. *Strategic Brand Communication Campaigns,* 5th ed. NY: McGraw-Hill, 1999.

Schultz, Majken, Mary Jo Hatch, and Mogens Holten Larsen, eds. *The Expressive Organization: Linking Identity, Reputation and the Corporate Brand.* NY: Oxford University Press, 2000.

Siegel, Alan. "Clarifying the Corporate Voice: The Imperative of the '90s." *Design Management Journal.* Winter 1994.

Technical Writing and Language Simplification

Burnett, Rebecca. *Technical Communication*, 6th ed. Boston: Wadsworth/ITP, 2005.

Harty, Kevin J. *Strategies for Business & Technical Writing*, 5th ed. Harcourt College Pub., 2005.

Johnson-Eilola, Johndan, and Stuart A. Selber, eds. *Central Works in Technical Communication*. NY: Oxford University Press, 2004.

Kaufer, David S., and Brian S. Butler. *Principles of Writing as Representational Composition*. Mahwah, NJ: Lawrence Erlbaum, 2000.

———. *Rhetoric and the Arts of Design*. Mahwah, NJ: Lawrence Erlbaum Associates, 1996.

Redish, Janice C. "Understanding Readers." Carol Barnum and Saul Carliner (eds.). *Techniques for Technical Communicators*. NY: Macmillan, 1993, 15–42.

Reynolds, Nedra, Patricia Bizzell, and Bruce Herzberg. *The Bedford Bibliography for Teachers of Writing*. 6th ed. NY: Bedford/St. Martin's, 2004.

Siegel, Alan. "Desperately Seeking Simplification." *Across the Board*, Nov/Dec 2001.

Graphic Design

Heller, Steven D., and Teresa Fernandes. *Becoming a Graphic Designer*. Hoboken, NJ: John Wiley &   Sons, Inc., 2006.

Heller, Steven, and Veronique Vienne, eds. *Citizen Designer: Perspectives on Design Responsibility*. NY: Watson-Guptill Publications, 2003.

Meggs, Phillip B., and Alison Purvis. *Meggs' History of Graphic Design*. NY: John Wiley & Sons, Inc., 2006.

Potter, Norman. *What Is a Designer: Things, Places, Messages*. NY: Princeton Architectural Press, 2002.

Print Production

Evans, Poppy. *Forms, Folds and Sizes: All the Details Graphic Designers Need to Know But Can Never Find*. London: Rockport Publishers, 2004.

Typography

Bellantoni, Jeff, and Matt Woolman. *Moving Type: Designing for Time and Space*. East Sussex, UK: RotoVision, 2000.

Cabarga, Leslie. *Logo, Font and Lettering Bible*. Cincinnati: HOW Design Books, 2004.

Ginger, E.M., and Erik Spiekermann. *Stop Stealing Sheep & Find Out How Type Works*. 2nd ed. Berkeley, CA: Adobe Press, 2002.

Lupton, Ellen. *Thinking with Type: A Critical Guide for Designers, Writers, Editors and Students*. NY: Princeton Architectural Press, 2004.

Grids

Elam, Kimberly. *Geometry of Design: Studies in Proportion and Composition*. NY: Princeton Architectural Press, 2001.

———. *Grid Systems: Principles of Organizing Type*. NY: Princeton Architectural Press, 2004.

Publications on and by Great Designers

Blackwell, Lewis. *David Carson 2ndsight: Grafik Design after the End of Print*. Universe Publishing, 1997.

Chermayeff, Ivan, Tom Geismar, and Steff Geissbuhler. *designing: Ivan Chermayeff, Tom Geismar, Steff Geissbuhler*. NY: Graphis Inc., November 2003.

Hall, Peter. *Sagmeister: Made You Look*. Booth-Clibborn, 2001.

Hall, Peter and Michael Bierut. *Tibor Kalman, Perverse Optimist*. NY: Princeton Architectural Press, 2000.

Hoffman, Armin. *Armin Hoffman: His Work, Quest and Philosophy*. Basel: Birkhauser (Architectural), 1991.

Kidd, Chip. *Chip Kidd: Book One: Work: 1986–2006*. NY: Rizzoli, 2005.

Mau, Bruce. *Life Style*. NY: Phaidon Press, 2005.

Meggs, Philip E. *Six Chapters in Design: Saul Bass, Ivan Chermayeff, Milton Glaser, Paul Rand, Ikko Tanaka, Henryk Tomaszewski*. San Francisco: Chronicle Books, 1997.

Rand, Paul. *Paul Rand: A Designer's Art.* New Haven, CT: Yale University Press, 2000.

Wozencroft, Jon. *The Graphic Language of Neville Brody* 2. Universe Publishing, 1996.

Compilations

Cranfield, Bill, ed. *Examining the Visual Culture of Corporate Identity.* Hong Kong: Systems Design Ltd., 2003.

Spencer, Herbert, and Rick Poynor. *Pioneers of Modern Typography: Revised Edition.* Cambridge, MA: The MIT Press, 2004.

Triggs, Teal. *Type Design: Radical Innovations and Experimentation.* NY: Collins Design, 2003.

Information Design

Heller, Steven. *Nigel Holmes: On Information Design.* NY: Jorge Pinto Books, 2006.

Lupton, Ellen J., and Abbott Miller. *Design Writing Research.* NY: Phaidon Press: 2000.

Tufte, Edward. *Envisioning Information.* Cheshire, CT: Graphics Press, 1990.

———. *The Visual Display of Quantitative Information*, 2nd ed. Cheshire, CT: Graphics Press, 2001.

Web Design

Curtis, Hillman. *Flash Web Design: The v5 Remix.* Berkeley, CA: New Riders Press, 2001.

Adobe Software

Cohen, Sandee, and Steve Werner. *Real World Adobe Creative Suite* 2. Berkeley, CA: Peachpit Press, 2006.

Author's Biography

Louis J Slovinsky retired as a corporate vice president from Time Warner Inc., where he directed corporate identity studies for Time Inc. and then Time Warner Inc. He was a brand analyst for Siegel & Gale and for Chermayeff & Geismar, and wrote freelance for Corporate Branding Partnership.

Notes

[1] Alan Siegel, interview by author, September 6, 2005.

[2] Ibid.

[3] Ibid.

[4] Ibid.

[5] Ibid.

[6] Internet Movie Database, *The Flamingo Kid*, http://www.imdb.com (accessed October 10, 2005).

[7] Jim Brown: Biography, http://www.sportsplacement.com/brownbio.htm (accessed April 30, 2006).

[8] Siegel interview, September 6, 2005.

[9] Ibid.

[10] *Cornell H.R: History and Mission*, http://www.ilr.cornell.edu/history (accessed September 28, 2005).

[11] Siegel interview, September 6, 2005.

[12] Ibid.

[13] Zeta Beta Tau was founded in 1898 as a Zionist youth society. Among its better known members are the late businessman Armand Hammer, comedian Robert Klein, attorney Robert Shapiro, journalist Mike Wallace, former Secretary of Commerce Mickey Kantor and musician Peter Yarrow of Peter, Paul and Mary, who is also a Cornell graduate. *ZBT History*, http://www.zbt.org (accessed September 28, 2005).

[14] Robert Dudnick, Los Angeles attorney, interview by author, December 5, 2005.

[15] Siegel interview, September 6, 2005.

[16] Ibid.

[17] Ibid.

[18] In *Rebel Without a Cause*, Dean drove a '49 black Mercury coupe. http://www.imdb.com (accessed March 28, 2006).

[19] Siegel interview, September 6, 2005.

[20] Ibid.

[21] Ibid.

[22] Ibid.

[23] Ibid.

[24] Ibid.

[25] Ibid.

[26] *M115 8-inch (203mm) Howitzer*, http://globalsecurity.org/military/systems/ground/m115.htm (accessed June 27, 2005).

[27] Lawrence M. Walsh, *The Fulda Gap*, July 2004, http://www.infosecuritymag.techtarget.com/ss/0,295796_iss426_art872,00.html (accessed April 5, 2006).

[28] Siegel interview, June 25, 2006.

[29] Ibid.

[30] *Design Archive Online: Alexey Brodovitch*, www.design.rit.edu/
Design/Biographies/brodovitch.html (accessed September 28,
2005).

[31] Siegel interview, September 6, 2005.

[32] *Masters of Photography: Lisette Model*, www.masters-photography.
com/M/model/model_articles1.html (accessed September 28,
2005).

[33] Gloria Siegel, wife of Alan Siegel, interview by author, September 25,
2006

[34] Ibid.

[35] Gloria Siegel interview, November 10, 2005.

[36] *History: NYCE*, www.hoovers.com/nyce (accessed November 10,
2005).

[37] James Kiewel, former executive vice president, Siegel & Gale, interview by author, November 16, 2005.

[38] Siegel interview, September 6, 2005.

[39] Kiewel interview, November 16, 2005.

[40] Siegel interview, July 6, 2006.

[41] Kiewel interview, November 16, 2005.

[42] Ibid.

[43] *Blog of Death: James Jordan Jr.*, February 9, 2004, www.blogofdeath.
com/archives (accessed October 27, 2005).

[44] Kiewel interview, November 16, 2005.

[45] Siegel interview, September 6, 2005.

[46] Richard Weiner, retired public relations executive, interview by author, November 11, 2005.

[47] Michael Kaufman, "J. Gordon Lippincott, 89, Dies; Pioneer Design
Consultant," *The New York Times*, May 7, 1998.

[48] Mirroring the consolidation of advertising firms to several global giants, the corporate identity business is now concentrated to a few
companies. Following an ownership change in 2003, Lippincott
& Margulies became Lippincott Mercer. Margulies died in 1989;
Lippincott withdrew from the business in 1996, and died two
years later.

[49] Milton Riback, *Name Changes*, Letter to the Editor, *The New York
Times*, May 29, 1987.

[50] Don Ervin, former Siegel & Gale design director, interview by author, October 21, 2005.

[51] Siegel interview, September 6, 2005.

[52] Ibid.

[53] Ervin interview, October 21, 2005. At Sandgren & Murtha, Siegel
helped develop the Major League Baseball trademark on the occa-
sion of baseball's centennial. According to Ervin, Juan Conception,
a young designer, drew the MLB image.

[54] David Davis, *"If West is the NBA's logo, should he be?"* http://www.
msn.foxsports.com/nba/story/5328860 (accessed March 14, 2006).

[55] Ibid.

[56] Ibid.

[57] Ervin interview, October 21, 2005.

[58] Siegel interview, December 8, 2005.

[59] Ibid.

[60] Wally Olins, *Corporate Identity* (New York: Thames & Hudson, Inc., 1994).

[61] James Salter, *Burning the Days* (New York: Random House, 1997).

[62] Siegel interview, July 6, 2006.

[63] Siegel interview, December 8, 2005.

[64] Siegel interview July 6, 2006.

[65] An advocate of managerial efficiency in government who had gained a worldwide reputation, the colorful Baldrige was a former ranch hand and professional team roper on the rodeo circuit. He was honored by the creation of the Malcolm Baldrige National Quality Awards in 1987, the year he died, at age 64, in a rodeo accident. *Malcolm Baldrige*, http://.en.wikipedia.org/wiki/Malcolm_Baldrige (accessed July 31, 2006).

[66] Charles Reisler, former partner of Siegel & Gale, interview by author, October 27, 2005.

[67] *3M Logo History*, http://www6.3M.com (accessed October 27, 2005).

[68] Ibid.

[69] Ibid.

[70] Ibid.

[71] Ibid.

[72] Siegel interview, July 6, 2006.

[73] Ibid.

[74] Siegel & Gale, *3M Case Study*, September 13, 2005.

[75] Reisler interview, October 27, 2005.

[76] Siegel interview, September 6, 2005.

[77] Siegel interview, July 6, 2006.

[78] Siegel e-mail to author, May 31, 2005.

[79] Kiewel interview, November 16, 2005.

[80] Ervin interview, October 21, 2005.

[81] Siegel interview, April 9, 2006.

[82] Alan Siegel speech, Town Hall of California, November 20, 1982, Reprinted in *Vital Speeches*, February 1, 1983.

[83] Ibid.

[84] Kenneth Morris, "Good Form: The Art of Document Design at Siegel & Gale," *Print Magazine*, January/February 1981.

[85] Kenneth Morris, former president of Siegel & Gale, interview by author, November 21, 2005.

[86] Alan Siegel, "To lift the curse of legalese—Simplify, Simplify," *Across the Board*, June 1977.

[87] Carl Felsenfeld, professor of law, Fordham University, interview by author, June 23, 2006.

[88] Alan Siegel, "Desperately Seeking Simplification," *Across the Board*, November/December 2001.

[89] Ibid.

[90] Siegel interview, June 6, 2006.

[91] Kenneth Morris, "Good Form: The Art of Document Design at Siegel & Gale," *Print Magazine*, January/February 1981.

[92] Morris interview, November 21, 2005.

[93] Weiner interview, November 11, 2005.

[94] Felsenfeld interview, June 23, 2006.

[95] Alan Siegel, Town Hall of California speech, November 20, 1982.

[96] The word "gobbledygook" was coined by Maury Maverick, Sr., in a memo dated March 30, 1944. As chairman of the U.S. Smaller War Plants Corporation during World War II, Maverick banned all "gobbledygook language" in official discourse. Tired of pompous language, the former member of the U.S. House of Representatives (Texas-D) declared that "anyone using the words *activation* or *implementation* will be shot." *Gobbledygook: Definition, Synonyms and Much More,* http://www/answers/com (accessed April 4, 2006).

[97] Joanne Locke, *A History of Plain Language in the United States Government* (2004), http://www.plainlanguage.gov/whatPL/history/locke.cfm (accessed October 15, 2005).

[98] Ibid.

[99] Janice Redish, president, Redish & Associates, interview by author, June 6, 2006.

[100] Ibid.

[101] Document design, simplified language, rhetoric and similar courses have spread to many colleges and universities, ranging form the University of Massachusetts and R.P.I. to the Universities of Washington and Southern California.

[102] Siegel interview, April 9, 2002.

[103] Erwin Steinberg, PhD, professor and former dean of the Humanities School, Carnegie Mellon, interview by author, October 14, 2005.

[104] Irene Etzkorn, senior consultant to Siegel & Gale, interview by author, October 12, 2005.

[105] Ibid.

[106] Ibid.

[107] Morris interview, October 28, 2005.

[108] Mary Dalrymple, *What ever happened to simplifying tax returns? AP,* April 15, 2006.

[109] Siegel interview, July 6, 2006.

[110] Ann Breaznell, former senior designer, Siegel & Gale, interview by author, April 8, 2006.

[111] Etzkorn interview, October 12, 2005.

[112] Gloria Siegel interview, September 25, 2006.

[113] Alan Siegel, "Clarifying the Corporate Voice: The Imperative of the '90s," *Design Management Journal,* Winter 1994.

[114] *Building Strong Brands with Distinctive Voices,* Siegel & Gale, 2004.

[115] Author's notes, employee training, Siegel & Gale, Fall 1994.

[116] Ibid.

[117] Wally Olins, the British branding consultant, is said to have been the first to plausibly compare the identity attributes of a corporation to a person.

[118] Siegel interview, July 6, 2006.

[119] Author's notes; see note 115.

[120] Alan Siegel, "Is Corporate Identity Dead?" speech to Conference Board, December 1992.

[121] *Corporate Voice*, written, designed and produced by Siegel & Gale, for a presentation sponsored by Crane Business Papers, June 15, 1989.

[122] Kelly Pender, *Glossary, Aristotle's Means of Persuasion*, http://wac.colostate.educ/books/lauer_invention/glossary.pdf. (accessed October 27, 2005).

[123] Kenneth M. Morris, *Communicating with Your Customers*, Rank Xerox symposium "The Importance of the Document in the Insurance World," June 3, 1992.

[124] Siegel & Gale, *Chubb Case Study*, September 13, 2005.

[125] Siegel and executives from advertising, direct marketing and public relations firms met with Xerox officials to present positioning statements they were asked to produce. After several show-and-tells, Siegel offered his: "The Document Company." "What the hell is that?" barked an adman. According to an inside source, Siegel retorted: "If you don't know, I'm not going to explain it to you, you horse's ass."

[126] Ibid.

[127] Dr. Thomas Walton, PhD, *Caterpillar: Working to Establish "One Voice,"* DMI Case Studies (DMI013), 2004.

[128] Ervin interview, October 21, 2005.

[129] *I.D.* magazine, January/February 2000.

[130] Howard Belk, Co-Managing Director – New York, Siegel & Gale, interview by author, August 9, 2006.

[131] Louis J. Slovinsky, "As a Name, Constellation Is a Black Hole," Canandaigua (NY). *Daily Messenger*, September 4, 2000.

[132] Siegel interview, May 1, 2006.

[133] *Rude Food*, http://.co.uk/sites/rudefood/index.php?page=food/spot-teddick.htm (accessed August 4, 2006).

[134] Siegel interview, May 1, 2006.

[135] Jeff Lapatine, Group Director, Naming & Brand Architecture, Siegel & Gale, interview by author, November 7, 2005.

[136] Gloria Siegel interview, July 25, 2006.

[137] Siegel interview, May 1, 2006.

[138] Ibid.

[139] Ibid.

[140] Alan Siegel, "Digital Voice," *Identity in a Digital World*, 1996.

[141] *Dot-Com Bubble*, http://en.wikipedia.org/wiki/Dot_Com_Bubble (accessed Aug. 11, 2006).

[142] Siegel interview, July 28, 2006.

[143] Siegel interview, June 5, 2006.

[144] Ibid.

[145] Ibid.

[146] Ibid.

[147] Ibid.

[148] Ibid.

[149] Tom Peters, "The Wow Project," *FastCompany,* p. 116, April 1999.

[150] Siegel interview, June 5, 2006.

[151] Ibid.

[152] Siegel interview, July 28, 2006.

[153] Siegel interview, June 5, 2006.

[154] David B. Srere, Co-Managing Director – New York, Siegel & Gale, interview by author, August 8, 2006.

[155] Siegel interview, December 8, 2005.

[156] Ironically, Samuel A. Maverick, the nineteenth-century Texas forebear of Maury Maverick, who coined the word "gobbledygook," chose not to brand his calves, which mingled with "branded" cattle on the open range. His willful act lives on in the term "maverick," to denote a nonconformist. (See endnote 96.)

[157] *The Compact Edition of the Oxford English Dictionary* (Oxford University Press, 1986), p. 264.

[158] Scott Bedbury with Stephen Fenichell, *A New Brand World* (New York: Viking, 2002), p. 15.

[159] Ibid.

[160] Siegel interview, December 8, 2005.

[161] Ibid.

[162] Lucas Conley, "Obsessive Branding Disorder," *FastCompany,* October 2005.

[163] Siegel interview, December 8, 2005.

[164] Patricia Deneroff, Group Director, Consulting, Siegel & Gale, interview by author, June 6, 2006.

[165] Srere interview, August 8, 2006.

[166] Deneroff interview, June 6, 2006.

[167] Ibid.

[168] Siegel interview, December 8, 2005.

[169] Deneroff interview, June 6, 2006.

[170] Srere interview, August 8, 2006.

[171] Ibid.

[172] T.S. Eliot, "The Hollow Men," *T.S. Eliot: The Complete Poems and Plays* (New York: Harcourt, Brace and Company, 1952), p. 58.

[173] www.siegelgale.com

[174] *Building Strong Brands with Distinctive Voices,* Siegel & Gale capabilities brochure, 2004.

[175] Ibid.

[176] The New School, "Eight Schools, One University," news release, August 2, 2005.

[177] Siegel interview, December 8, 2005.

[178] Ibid.

[179] Ibid.

[180] Siegel & Gale's Brand Voice Books, or Voice Resources Guides, introduce employees to the concept of Brand Voice—the tone, manner and style of its communications. When Brand Voice is unified, all of its communications share a familiar spirit, feeling and attitude. The governing thesis is that the discovery of

a Promise (brand promise), together with Behavior (brand attributes), and Presentation (brand voice) can result in a unified "brand platform." Brand Books challenge employees to think about these principles and act in ways that reinforce the brand.

[181] *Building Strong Brands with Distinctive Voices,* Siegel & Gale capabilities brochure, 2004.

[182] Interview with Siegel, April 23, 2006.

[183] Ibid.

[184] Ibid.

[185] Ibid.

[186] Ibid.

[187] Ibid.

[188] Ibid.

[189] Julius Winfield Erving II, aka Dr. J., "operated" with supreme success on the basketball court, winning three scoring titles in five ABA season, and elected five times in eleven seasons to NBA All-Star teams, as well as to the Naismith Memorial Hall of Fame (1993). http://nba.com/history/players/erving_bio.html (accessed April 29, 2006).

[190] Reminiscence of Claude Singer, former Siegel & Gale executive, February 26, 2006.

[191] Reisler interview, October 27, 2005.

[192] Herb Schmertz, retired director of Mobil Corporation, interview by author, February 14, 2006.

[193] Eva Hardy, senior vice president, Dominion Resources, interview by author, March 6, 2006.

[194] Harry Petchesky, New York attorney, interview by author, November 10, 2005

[195] Gloria Siegel interview, September 25, 2006.

[196] Ray Olson, *Booklist* editorial review, *Step Right This Way: The Photographs of Edward J. Kelty,* (Barnes & Noble, 2002), http://www.amazon.com (accessed April 29, 2006).

[197] Siegel interview, April 23, 2006.

Index

Printed in the United States
65783LVS00003B/183